# THE PERFECT COUNTRY COTTAGE

# THE PERFECT
# COUNTRY COTTAGE

## BILL LAWS

### CONRAN OCTOPUS

*To Abby*

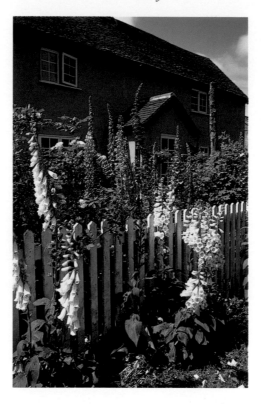

*Project Editor* JOANNA BRADSHAW
*Art Editor* MERYL LLOYD
*Picture Research* ABIGAIL AHERN
*Production Controller* JULIA GOLDING

First published in Great Britain in 1993 by
Conran Octopus Limited
37 Shelton Street
London WC2H 9HN

Text © Bill Laws 1993
Design and layout © Conran Octopus Limited 1993

The right of Bill Laws to be identified as Author of this work has been asserted by him in accordance with the Copyright, Designs and Patents Act 1988.

British Library Cataloguing-in-Publication Data
A catalogue record for this book is available from the British Library

ISBN 1 85029 530 1

Typeset by Servis Filmsetting Limited
Printed in China

# CONTENTS

*Introduction*
## A SIMPLE FORM OF LIVING
7

*Chapter One*
## FIRST IMPRESSIONS
19

*Chapter Two*
## HEART OF THE HOME
43

*Chapter Three*
## ROOMS FOR LIVING
65

*Chapter Four*
## SLEEPING QUARTERS
89

*Chapter Five*
## THE COTTAGE GARDEN
113

*Chapter Six*
## A COUNTRY HARVEST
133

INDEX 142    ACKNOWLEDGMENTS 144

# A SIMPLE FORM OF LIVING

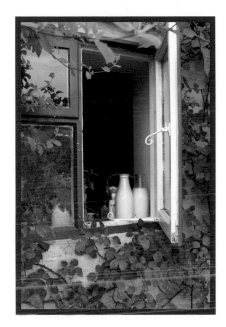

What is a perfect cottage? And how best can a traditional cottage feel be imparted to a not-so-perfect old building? In the following chapters we explore the origins and sheer variety of the simple country home, from Cornwall to Connecticut, Greece to Grenoble, and offer practical suggestions on how to recreate a country atmosphere in a house that is at home with its local landscape.

More often than not, the exterior of a cottage will offer a few visual clues as to what kind of interior treatment it should be given. For instance, the kitchen of a simple flint cottage with small windows would not benefit from the addition of gleaming stainless steel fitted units — the clash of materials would be too much. Likewise, a light and airy barn conversion would look stark and uninviting if filled with small, low pieces of furniture that did not capitalize on its inherently tall ceilings. The overriding consideration when furnishing a traditional vernacular home should always be to remain faithful to the original structure by making a warm, comfortable interior that does not destroy the original character of the building.

LOCAL DISTINCTIVENESS

This Irish longhouse in County Galway with its stubby chimney, slurried slate roof and bright whitewashed face makes a distinctive contribution to the look of the surrounding landscape.

# PERFECT COTTAGES

The concept of the perfect country cottage is one of infinite variety and style. The cottage – a small house which fits harmoniously into its rural setting and whose unselfconscious interior is cosy and welcoming – may be a limestone worker's dwelling in the Cotswolds, a timber-framed house in New England or a tiny stone and thatch shelter in Ireland. Traditionally, these homes were built by local builders using indigenous materials to blend effortlessly into the surrounding natural landscape.

To our modern eyes, the most evocative and atmospheric country homes are those which have retained their original character while having been sympathetically restored using salvaged or carefully reproduced elements such as fireplaces, beams, exposed brick walls, doors, windows and shutters.

From the time when people first settled the land to the contemporary urban longing for an uncomplicated country existence, the unpretentious rural dwelling has retained firm favour in the popular imagination.

## STYLE VARIETY

*The hard lines of Brittany's indigenous granite are softened on this cottage (above) by the flow of the reed thatch roof which sits above the small dormer window. Brick and timber are the basic materials for this Shaker-style home in the United States (right). Locally-made brick forms the fireproof hearth and chimney indoors, while outdoors, clapboard is used to face and protect the building's façade.*

# EXTERIORS

Different people have different ideas about what constitutes the perfect country cottage. For a modern family of Boston back-to-the-landers perfection could mean an ecologically sound timber-framed cabin standing on fertile soil and close, but not too close, to the village school and grocery store. Their counterparts in a Stockholm suburb might prefer a user-friendly small house with a distinctly country feel and all the amenities of modern life. In Milan, meanwhile, the idyllic retreat for city-weary people might be a winter chalet high up on an isolated mountain pass.

The common thread running through these lives is the desire to live in simple, country-style surroundings, in harmony with the rural environment. This universal desire

knows no geographical boundaries and has given us a rich variety of vernacular building styles.

Take the reed-thatched and whitewashed Camargue cabane and the snow white clapboard of a small Massachusetts farmhouse. Both employ the three basic materials common to all cottage building – timber, earth and stone – yet the two buildings are as far apart in looks as they are in distance. Designs vary from country to country, region to region, even from village to village. Among the apple orchards and cattle pastures of French Normandy one village is dominated by low, long houses with a crest of lilies on their thatched ridges; in the next village sturdy limestone houses with dark slate roofs predominate because of the local abundance of these materials. Before cheap, mass produced materials became widely available, each parish built its homes from whatever lay close to hand. Function rather than fashion ruled the vernacular look.

But the see-saw world of style and design has regularly paid homage to the small country dwelling. Before losing her head on Doctor Guillotin's machine, the 17th-century French queen Marie Antoinette eschewed the glitz of Versailles Palace life for the pseudo-country style of Le Hameau. Across the channel in England, William Morris' contempt for conspicuous consumption and opulent artificiality brought about the Arts and Crafts movement, and a renewed appreciation of hand-crafted furniture and fittings.

ATTENTION TO DETAIL

*The softwoods of Eastern Europe can be cut and carved into elaborate decorative forms as on this building in Czechoslovakia (above). In Normandy, by contrast, the timber frame of this vernacular farmhouse creates its own decorative pattern (left).*

At the end of the twentieth century, individual craftspeople are once more in demand, among them woodturners, carpenters and stonemasons. At the same time, many exterior vernacular features such as half-timbering, dormer windows, half-hipped roofs, country kitchens and ledge-and-brace doors have become standard elements in the design of countless housing estates. The cottage tradition lives on.

# COTTAGES AND THE LANDSCAPE

Why does a Cumbrian cottage with its black stone and green slate roof differ so dramatically from a simple Mediterranean house with walls of whitewashed rubble and a roof of Roman tiles? The answer is the vernacular building tradition. Vernacular is the Latin word for a slave born in his master's house and thus a native. Vernacular buildings are those that are native to their own province.

Such folk buildings were among the earliest forms of architecture and it is the tried and tested methods of vernacular building design that have endured long enough to inform the design process of many a modern skyscraper. But a legacy of traditional buildings survives around the world: red, Roman-tiled farmhouses in southern France; reed and timber marshland huts in Italy's Caserta region and settlers' timber cottages on the east coast of America.

These buildings mirror the underlying groundstones, slipping inconspicuously into the surrounding countryside and colouring our judgement about what looks right and proper in the countryside. As William Wordsworth put it, they 'may rather be said to have grown than to have been erected – to have risen by an instinct of their own, out of the native rock – so little is there in them of formality, such is their wildness and beauty.'

Wordsworth was referring to his native Cumbrian cot, sheltering in the lea of some craggy fell, its rough stone walls bright with whitewash, and its two tubby chimneys poking out from a roof of Westmoreland slate. He might have said the same thing about a Finnish log cabin, sheathed in weathered, vertical boards, its open-air gallery looking out across a vast area of birchwood scrub. The two scenes are as purposeful as they are picturesque, for each building evolved to make the best use of local climate and topography.

### VERNACULAR RESPONSE

*In the English lakelands (right), rugged Cumbrian stone is used to build farms and cottages. A French farmhouse in the Vallée du Var (top left) boasts a roof of Roman tiles, or tuile á canal. Where local stone was poor, tin and timber were called into service (centre left). A neat cabin on the island of Grenada (bottom left) displays a colourful exterior.*

# LOCAL MATERIALS

## BUILT BY HAND

*A growing awareness of vernacular furnishings, fixtures and features such as those at Kennixton (above right), an early seventeenth-century farmhouse rebuilt at the Welsh Folk Museum in South Wales, has led to a growing interest in their care and preservation.*

*Vernacular buildings were traditionally constructed as a direct response to regional climate and conditions, without the aid of architects. These decorated timber homes beside a Romanian road (below right) reflect local decorative building traditions and a sensitive use of colour.*

## MATERIAL VALUE

*The arrival of cheap, mass-produced building materials finally brought the vernacular tradition, typified by the beautiful beehived roofs on this Dordogne farmhouse (above left), to a close.*

*New ideas and new materials such as the gable end hearths and chimney pots on this Hebridean croft (below left) gradually filtered through to remote regions.*

*Increasingly, homes like these are being discreetly brought up to date indoors despite the conservation of practical exterior features such as the thatch roof.*

# RESTORING ORIGINAL FEATURES

● Tracing the history of your home can be an absorbing task. Try to establish the original layout of the cottage. Built-up doorways or the remains of an old arch in a wall are useful clues, while a stone lower floor with a half-timbered upper floor suggests that the second storey was a later addition to the building.

● Most small country houses functioned as both home and workplace. The original layout will often reveal its former use: an open-plan upper floor lit by unusually large windows could indicate a cottage weaving gallery; a slab-floored cellar with a drain down the centre may be the remains of a wine or beer store from a former inn.

● Look at the exterior materials; handmade bricks are irregular in both shape and colour, while roman bricks, still in use today, are twice the length and half the thickness of a conventional brick. Check whether the outside facing material of brick, boarding or render conceals older material.

● Although most roofs will have been stripped and replaced every century, they are a useful key to the past. Explore the roof space where former timbers will be retained; smoke blackened timbers indicate an old hall house, once open up to the roof.

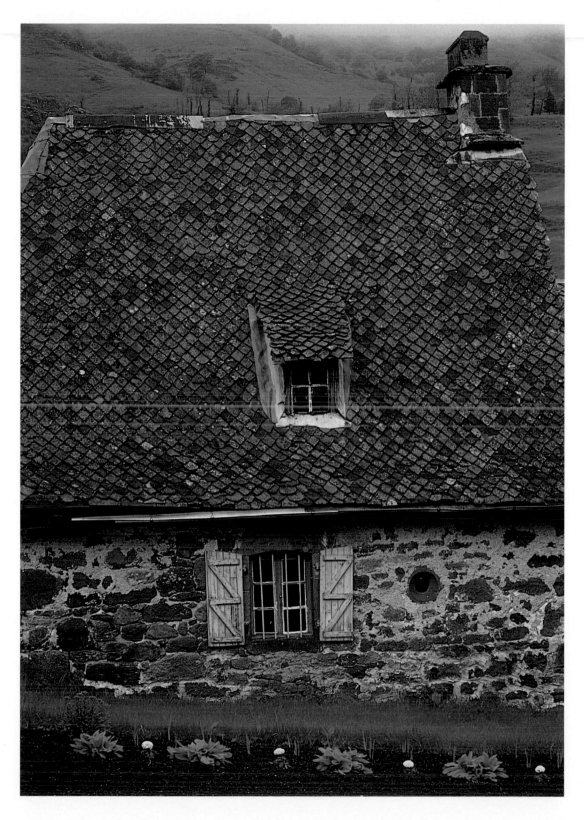

● *Documentary evidence on small, rural homes is often rudimentary but parish records, early maps and estate journals are good starting places. If your home was once a working building like a mill, farmhouse, café or smithy, there is a better chance of it having been recorded somewhere.*

● *Datestones and commemorative inscriptions are helpful although they were often inscribed to celebrate a rebuilding rather than the founding of the cottage. Tracing back the original cottage name can also provide pertinent clues as to its origins.*

## CLUES TO THE PAST

*The cart doors, stone slate roof and old-fashioned chimney, built before chimney pots came into fashion, all provide clues to the age of this cottage (opposite top).*

*Never judge a house by its roof — the steep pitch of the clay tile roof on this former farmhouse in the Massif Central region of France suggests an original covering of thatch (left).*

*A guide to the original purpose of a country home often lies in specialist outbuildings such as this circular hop kiln and adjoining cooling house (opposite bottom) in Kent, England.*

# FIRST IMPRESSIONS

*Glimpsing a country cottage for the first time can be a joyous experience. Greeted by graceful, ancient roses ranged round a snug porch, wisteria draped sineously from a gabled portico, or walls washed in warm terracotta, who would not be completely consumed by a delightful sense of expectation?*

*Country cottages blend into the landscape without being inconspicuous, they rise proudly from the earth which, more often than not, fashioned their framework and shaped their exterior.*

*Such traditional buildings have often stood their ground unchanged for centuries, having become part and parcel of the local culture.*

*Despite apparent similarities, no two cottages are exactly the same. Each has reflected the individuality of its inhabitants for a century or so and a careful appraisal of all its inherent exterior details, whether they be original features or unsuccessful replacements, needs to be carried out before sympathetic restoration work begins.*

### SHELTERING THATCH

*A glorious fusion of wildflowers and herbs provides a rich and colourful welcome at this English country cottage near Sidbury in Dorset. A brick-built extension has been sympathetically grafted on to the older, whitewashed part of the house by carrying the rolling thatch across both roofs.*

# MAKING AN ENTRANCE

The quiet calm of a cottage approach, with its sea of proud, fragrant hollyhocks and foxgloves, or a façade of brilliant white stone and crisply contrasting black-painted woodwork certainly lends credence to the idea that country living is clean and healthy and good for the soul.

A traditional cottage is usually sited on a weathertight plot to make the best use of all the elements. Hedged against cold winds and open to the sunny south, a kitchen garden was often to be found, set close to the house so as to shorten the regular journeys between the herb bed and the cooking pot, not to mention the frequent journeys between the water supply and the tin bath.

Any path was purely for pedestrians, but for the modern cottage a driveway is just as essential. The appearance of bulldozer tracks through a cottage hedgebank is one of the early warning signs that an old house is about to be brought up to date. The drive which thrusts its way to the cottage door like a miniature motorway is an ominous sign: is the old house being bullied unceremoniously into the twentieth century? Or will the character of the building and its furnishings be tastefully retained? The entranceway to a country cottage and the first impressions it bestows on a visitor is as important to its overall character as is a careful and sensitive choice of furniture and fittings indoors.

WHITEWASHED STONE

*A mossy thatch roof (left) butts up to plain stone parapets on this whitewashed cottage. Rainwater gutters were not traditionally applied to thatched houses, so a black tar surround was used to protect the base of the walls from water splashing against them.*

WATERPROOF WEATHERBOARD

*Yellow flag irises (above) stand sentinel at the gateway leading to a seventeenth-century whipple house near Ipswich, Massachusetts. The original timber for the shingle roof and clapboard will have been obtained from local woodlands.*

# BEATING A PATH

Before the advent of the automobile, the cottage lay as close to the thoroughfare as a goose to its down. The small country house showed its best profile to the roadside as visitors stepped off the curtilage straight into the front door. It was a necessarily short journey, given that everything from the annual apple crop to the daily bucket of water had to be carried over the threshold. But, as passing traffic began to disrupt this previously peaceful state of affairs, the cottager closed off the front door and ran a path round to the back, making an entranceway at the rear.

Since fruit and flowers grew round the back, the idea of being lead up these garden paths was more a pleasure than a deceit. River gravel, broken roof slates, stone slabs and brick or pounded dirt were variously employed to pave a winding way through flower borders and herb beds to the back door. On the cottage itself, damp-proof courses were rare and rain-water gutters rudimentary or non-existent; on the earth or cob cottage, a well-tended grit or gravel path was a necessity since the skirting path drained away surface water.

In the timber-rich territories of Scandinavia or among the forests of North America, a plank and pole boardwalk carried the visitor to the cabin doorstep. Not only did the creaking pathway keep the housewife's skirts out of the winter mud, its echoing footfalls also warned her of approaching guests. In southern Europe, a visitor's clogs were more likely to resound against compacted road stone or granite cobbles along paths which lead to the terrace or patio, where the al fresco life of the Mediterranean household rumbled amiably along from generation to generation.

GARDEN PATH

*A studded oak door in Hartland, Devon (above left) is entirely in keeping with the stone doorway and slate steps, while a timber-clad porch protects a plain ledge-and-brace door (above right).*

*Framed by tree boughs, this wide brick path meanders gently to the doorstep (right). To create a similar effect, use old, irregular bricks and bed them in sand or earth. They will gradually slip and settle into comfortable undulations.*

# PAINTED EXTERIORS

Cottages and country houses have presented a painted face to the world from the earliest of times, partly to make them stand out amongst the greenery of the countryside and partly to weatherproof them from the elements.

Whitewash made with chalk dust, size and milk was the most common treatment, sometimes confined to front walls or doorways alone, but earth-colour washes were common throughout Europe from medieval times. Bright yellows, blues, burnt umbers and ochres were drawn from local materials, and whole villages reflected the colour of their surroundings. In Rustrel in southern France, houses were painted with red pigment from the neighbouring ground-stones, while in Saffron Walden in eastern England, homes were coloured using the saffron crocus grown in the region.

White lead paints were popular treatments for window frames, while exposed softwood timbers were picked out in darker blacks and blues, primarily for protection. The habit of painting oak blue, brown or the black so typical of middle England was more decorative than practical, since the natural silver-grey oak would season like iron and outlast its surrounding wattle and daub.

Choosing exterior house colours today is less a question of available colours – the range of external paints and pigments is almost limitless – but more one of available light. The faded pinks and yellow ochres of a Mediterranean fishing village look at home in the crisp, bright winter morning light. But such colours would not travel well to the honey-gold limestone cottages of the French Dordogne or to the English Cotswolds.

Be guided both by the age of your home and by local tradition. In the Labourd region of the Basque country, where threads of red pimentos drying in the sun decorate the house walls, timberwork looks spectacular painted in strident reds and greens against a sparkling whitewash; in western Ireland, the inhabitants are ready to risk a sharp yellow or red ground floor against a white painted upper floor and to paint the doors and windows in cheerfully contrasting lime green.

Experiment with different colours on a tracing of the

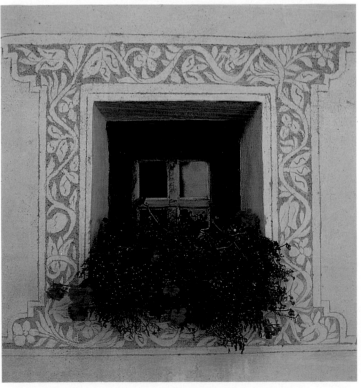

cottage drawn from a large-scale photograph. Having made your choice, remember to use permeable paints which will let bare stone or brickwork breathe. Repeating the wall colours on doors, windows and shutters can work well on clapboard buildings, while contrasting tones such as red window and door frames against stone or brick, or black frames against a whitewashed wall, can be effective.

Exterior ornamentation was rarely found on the unfussy exteriors of most country cottages, so care should be taken to preserve unusual features that are still intact, such as datestones, carvings or wall paintings.

### MATCHING PAIR

*As a general rule, the smaller the window, the older the house. These two windows (far left above) on a cottage built of bare earth and thatched with raw reeds are protected by the deep eaves of the roof.*

### LEAN-TO LOOK

*The convention of building windows into a cottage as the house rose was not followed on log cabins (far left below). Instead window and door openings were sawn through after the walls had been built, hence the asymetrical appearance of this pair of windows on a log house.*

### CLASSIC FRANCE

*The characteristic Mediterranean window is narrow, deep and sheltered by old wooden shutters. Here (above left) the window surrounds are picked out in pink against the whitewashed walls. A window box filled with petunias completes the scene.*

### SWISS SGRAFFITI

*This window set deep in the wall of a Swiss building in the Eurgadine region (below left) is surrounded by sgraffiti decoration. Features like these, though more common in central and highland Europe, are rare, so they should be preserved and maintained.*

# FRAMING THE VIEW

Until the nineteenth century, the durable wooden shutter was once the only answer to letting in the best, and keeping out the worst, of the weather. The clatter of little timber doors being opened or closed has echoed across the continents at sunrise and sunset ever since.

Early shutters comprised freestanding wooden frames which were lifted into place at sunset. But by the eighteenth century they were hinged on metal pins that had been driven into the wall, fitted with louvred sections to circulate fresh air or, a favourite custom in Alpine regions, pierced with a decorative eye-hole, shaped like the native fir tree.

And by the nineteenth century, most shutters closed against glazed windows. Initially glass was too expensive for the average cottager; those who could afford window panes across their 'windholes' regarded them as furniture and floorboards and took all with them when they moved. Although the Romans had manufactured glass, the conventional cottage window held the elements at bay with anything but glass: slivers of pale, thin horn; alabaster; oiled paper; even the placenta of cattle or horses was used instead.

When affordable glass arrived on the market, it was cut into small diamond shapes then set in lead, like many church windows. Cheaper sheet glass lead to the Dutch-designed sliding sash windows spreading across Europe in the early nineteenth century, while the horizontal sliding sash appeared on low-browed cottages that featured two tiny windows tucked under the eaves. A century later, cast-iron casements were popular until they too were replaced by modern timber casements.

Redundant hop kilns, old boathouses, workshops, cow sheds and hay barns have all been converted into cottages and many have distinctive windows which tell something of their past. Typical examples are pitching eyes set in the gable wall of a building and used to pitchfork winter supplies of hay into the old barn, or small oval or semi-circular openings set under the eaves to circulate fresh air around the loft.

Cottage windows and other features like them are the eyes of the house. Replace them with wide expanses of toughened glass, mock-Georgian units or aluminium frames and it has the same visual impact as removing the back lawn and relaying plastic grass. However, by returning windows to their original style, by having them specially made and by using sympathetic window treatments on the inside, you can restore rather than ruin a traditional cottage.

As a rough guide, the older the house, the smaller the window and diminutive windows restrict both the light and the view. The conventional four-paned window can be replaced with a deeper nine- or twelve-paned frame and the heat loss of the increased area reduced by the addition of secondary glazing or indoor shutters.

Old windows are often made of a superior hardwood and can be given a new lease of life by replacing rotten sections, usually the sill, and painting the repair. New wooden casements must be painted or, to reduce maintenance, treated with a stain. Pick out frames and sills in white or pale colours — dark colours tend to demote and camouflage the windows, especially against shadowy stone buildings — and use a pale colour inside to reflect more light into the rooms. French windows which open out onto a patio or garden add a sense of space to a room and allow light to flood in. In warmer weather they can be left open during the day to let fresh air circulate through the room. On the inside, hang generous fabric curtains or old lace, rather than venetian blinds, which would look too harsh.

## VERNACULAR SIMPLICITY

*This small but beautiful window is set into a limewashed wall which nestles under a wooden shingle roof. Metal brackets have been used to reinforce the opening and extend the life of the old casement.*

# SHUTTERS

- Shutters are an important vernacular detail, exhibiting both the aesthetic and practical nature of traditional building techniques.

- The metal hooks from which shutters hang are weak points in the design and will need replacing from time to time.

- Recycle old metalwork handles, hooks and bars which are often cast in unusual designs such as a clenched fist or open hand. Clean the metal with a sand blaster or wire brush and paint it with a protective coat of metal paint.

- Timber shutters will need to be repainted from time to time. Rub down the old paint, clean the wood with white spirit and repaint. Modern stains and microporous paints which allow the wood to breath are preferable on new softwoods.

- Using louvred external shutters as ornamentation on Northern cottages can look out of place. They are better sited indoors in cold climates.

## OPEN HOUSE

This wall clock and shutters (above left), are typical of a high alpine village.

The louvred and panelled shutters on these cottage walls (far left below, left, and right) filter light and fresh air into the interior.

# DOORS

The door is the key exterior element of any house. It is the first feature people notice and, whether they strike the grinning devil doorknocker or lift the latch, the door is the first device they use, so first impressions count.

During the eighteenth century, doors were still so small that they would barely reach above the shoulders of a modern-day teenager. Small but heavy, these wooden doors were hung on strap hinges from proper door frames, fitted with ornamental metal latches and, after the invention of the concealed mortice lock, very occasionally armed with a lock. Like the modern burglar alarm, the presence of a prominent keyhole suggested there might be something worth stealing in the cottage. There rarely was, and until the late nineteenth century locks were only significant as a sign of social status rather than as security devices.

Mass-produced panelled doors eventually came into general use in the nineteenth century, when the solid ledge-and-brace door was relegated to the woodshed or cut down to fit a bedroom. A similar fate befell both the door divided vertically down the middle and the useful heck-door or stable door, divided horizontally and used to let light and air into the kitchen, while keeping stray hens and the farmhouse dog out. Both types are now in regular use again in many renovated country cottages.

External doors these days should be made of hardwood and furnished with door handles and knockers of painted cast iron rather than brass or aluminium. In some cases, a repaired door is superior to a brand new door, which is likely to be flimsily made and expensive, or both. The first signs of wear on an old door appear around the bottom weatherboard and on the lower panels. They can be repaired easily by jointing-in new sections.

Traditionally, it was common practise throughout rural Europe to pick out the doorframe in whitewash, a technique which served the practical purpose of guiding the smallholders back to their thresholds on dark, moonless nights. Where the door and window frames are white, the door itself can take a contrastingly bright colour.

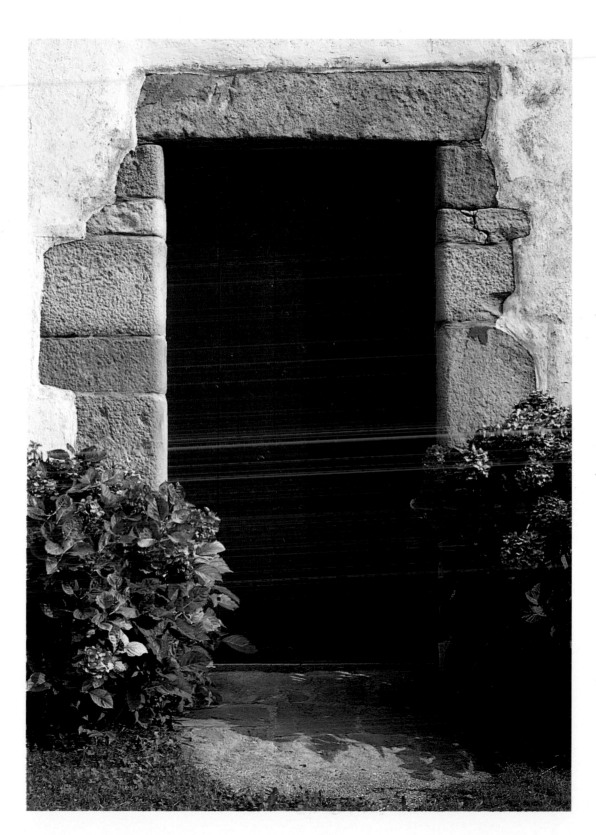

## OGEE ARCH

*Ornamentation on old country cottages was often confined to a simple arched doorway (opposite left). Four quarter lights have been added to the door to lighten the hallway beyond.*

## GREY SLATE FACE

*The plain panelled door on this Welsh cottage (opposite right) is surrounded by a sea of slate. Slates or tiles form a weatherproof finish to west-facing walls.*

## CELTIC CUSTOMS

*The habit of leaving the granite doorway free of whitewash, was common all along the western seaboard of Europe and focused attention on the central painted front door ( left ).*

# PORCHES AND VERANDAS

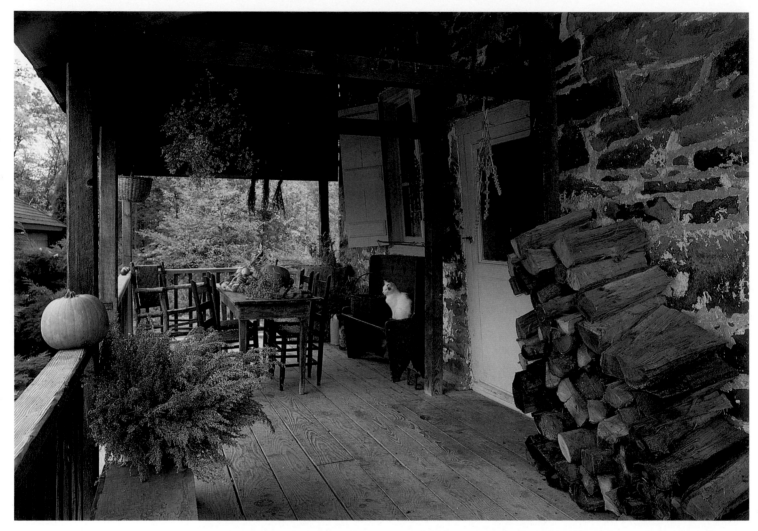

The Southern terrace, patio or veranda is as necessary to the well-being of a householder as the shaded porch is to those in the North. Verandas were traditionally adopted by British colonials to make the most of the outdoors without having to face glaring sunlight or suffer heatstroke. American settlers also found them useful, since the addition of a generous timber deck could double the living space of a classic country cottage. Unlike the Spanish, who preferred the Moorish privacy of an inner courtyard, the American settlers, like their Scandinavian forefathers, liked to sit and watch the world go by from their front porches.

The veranda has always been an intrinsic part of the house, sheltered by a shingle roof and sometimes enclosed by ivy-clad latticework. But the Northern porch was often an afterthought. Even in the bleakest, most windswept regions of western England, outside porches did not appear until the end of the sixteenth century.

On larger cottages and farmhouses, the porch might be a two-storey edifice, the upper storey incorporating a cold larder or spare bed chamber, lit by an oriel window. On smaller, single-storey cottages such as the granite Devon longhouse, the porch was built as broad as an ox, with flanking walls deep enough to deflect side winds. Often a stone or slate bench was inserted into the east wall to catch the late-day sun.

Midway between north and south, in the predictably

damper climates of the west coasts of France, Britain and Ireland, a simpler solution was the door hood, made from thatch and timber or a creeper-laden trellis beneath a lead or slate hood. In Brittany, a favourite late nineteenth-century design was a door hood of glass and wrought-iron, also adopted to shelter the family headstone in the local village graveyard.

These days, outdoors leads indoors through a hall. The 'hall' in medieval times was the main room of a building where the inhabitants lived, ate and slept while a 'porch' was an inner, draught-proof room between the door and the hall. In the traditional longhouse design, cattle and kin were separated from each other by a cross passage running from the front to the back doors. Eventually the passage was closed off to create a storage space for the clutter of waterproofs and galoshes.

## SHADE AND SHELTER

*A wide and weathertight timber deck beneath an extension to a house roof provides extra living and storage space (opposite).*

*Trailing wisteria and a simple porch hood screen the face of this brick and flint cottage (top left).*

*The materials used to add a broad porch to this half-timbered house faithfully follow the older timber framing with brick infill (above left).*

*The L-shaped corner of this American clapboard house is an ideal location for an open veranda, providing a place to sit, eat and relax (above).*

# HALLWAYS

A north- or west-facing hall will let in the weather and let out the heat every time the door is opened, while the door leading to a south-facing hall will tend to be left open on sunny days. Since all house traffic will constantly pass through it, the cottage hall needs to be light, hardwearing and uncluttered.

Where space is at a premium, and the hall has been built merely as a convention to some forgotten fashion, the room can be removed altogether. In northern areas a weathertight porch would suffice, while in warm southern regions an open trellised porch would work well.

Natural daylight is the ideal lighting for a hall. In the absence of a window, consider using a half-glazed door, veiled with a thin curtain for privacy. Alternatively, build a fanlight above the door.

Hardwearing floors, such as tiles, stone flags or wooden boards are preferable to carpeting since, in the winter months, much of the outside will inevitably find its way inside.

Hall walls tend to suffer more than their fair share of scuff marks. Washable wallpapers provide some protection, but opt for light colours to avoid creating a gloomy entrance.

## WELCOME HOME

*The glimpse of an upstairs rooms, a view of the Tuscan hills and a welcoming tray of fruit lend this farmhouse a warm and hospitable feel (opposite).*

*The pale colours in this Umbrian farmhouse hall (left) have been carried up across the ceiling to reflect the natural daylight flooding in from a central window. Simple ornaments, a delightful small table and chair and an enchanting frieze make the room both useful and welcoming.*

*Simple flagstones, limewashed walls and bare ceiling timbers act as a backcloth to old, flamboyantly painted, vertically divided doors set deep in the wall (above).*

# HALL FURNITURE

The transition area from outdoors to indoors should be made warm and welcoming: crossing the threshold though the stable-type door onto the broad-timbered floor of this Polish house (right), with its bright rag throws and warm red paintwork, provides an agreeable encounter.

A pleasantly cool reception awaits the visitor to this Greek cottage (far left above). The low doorway is a familiar feature in traditional country homes, built in the days when the average height of the occupants would have been much lower than today.

A Scandinavian hall provides decoration in the form of painted geometric shapes on the walls and swirling designs on the floor (above left).

White entranceways like these (far left below) which reflect the maximum amount of light into what would otherwise be a dim and gloomy hall passage, work well in any climate. Provide a Shaker pegrail and some interesting hangers, and you can create an inviting hallway in the most spartan of country houses.

There is a minimum of fuss or furniture to meet the visitor in this tiled Greek entrance hall (below left). Just a cane-backed rocking chair, an ornamental pot and a plain back door framed by bare granite adorn the space.

# Chapter Two

# HEART OF THE HOME

The country kitchen has always been the traditional heart of the home. Centuries ago it was the place where the day's business was discussed over breakfast, where families and their workers shared their meals and where, in the evening, the household gathered by the fireside to take stock of the day's events.

After an uncomfortable period during the 1950s when the kitchen was seen as inferior to the more formal parlour, the classic country kitchen, with its natural materials, spacious seating and informal atmosphere has returned to popular favour with a vengeance.

But the kitchen has also had to react to the development of high-tech labour-saving devices such as washing machines and microwave ovens, refrigerators and built-in ovens. All bulky items that have threatened to destroy the character of many older kitchens, turning them in to push-button factories of barefaced steel and clinical plastic. It need not be so. Judicious planning and an inventive use of cupboard space to disguise equipment can mean you are free to recreate an informal atmosphere at the heart of the home.

AQUA WOOD

*Imaginatively painted cupboards ranged along one wall make this a practical but comfortable working kitchen that doubles as a family room.*

# WORKING KITCHENS

The country kitchen is often torn between convenience and convention. The conventional necessities have always been a dependable source of heat, water and storage space, while the conveniences depend upon the technology of the time. The current trend towards fast food and a kitchen cleansed of the smell of cooking has made a god of convenience and a devil of convention. But pristine and clinical fitted units are gradually giving way to individual, painted dressers and shelves; microwaves are being banished to painted cupboards; and ovens, dishwashers and washing machines discreetly tucked away behind wooden doors.

In medieval times, the country kitchen was both workroom and living room, cramped and uncomfortable. Today, as labour-saving devices have taken the physical

hardship out of preparing and cooking food, the kitchen has once again become the heart of the country home, a place to meet, eat and live in comfort, with enough space for tables and chairs, as well as a food preparation area.

An original inglenook is an ideal place for the solid-fuel stove which heats the water, the food and the room. Alternatively, a built-in oven and separate hob can be placed between the sink and the refrigerator, with useful work surfaces and cupboards placed in between. To avoid the uniform look of the store-bought kitchen, try customizing wooden units by painting or stencilling them in different colours and replacing door handles. Alternatively, ask a local carpenter to construct the carcassing or cupboard supports to suit your work surfaces and clad them in doors made up from reclaimed timbers, stained or painted to harmonize with your favourite dresser or fireside settle.

Many cottage kitchens have been enlarged by knocking through a wall to give a generous-sized living area. Where once the larder or dairy stood, utility rooms have been created, allowing the freezer and washing machine, a useful but noisy appliance, to be moved from the kitchen.

The kitchen table, chairs and work surfaces should blend in with the original room. Opt for worktops of natural materials such as slate, tiles, marble or wood, and back them with a frieze of handmade tiles. Position a mismatching row of shelves made from left-over wood above them.

Avoid the regimented style of a completely fitted kitchen and enjoy matching natural textures and materials; an

earthenware jug filled with wooden spoons and rolling pins, a bread crock and wicker bowls of fruit and vegetables, old butcher's hooks hung with weathered copper pans and utensils, all sit happily in a country kitchen. Store food mixers and liquidizers in an old pie cupboard or on the lower shelves of the dresser, and the result will be a more harmonious working atmosphere.

### HEARTH AND HOME

*A traditional cooking fire with its fire bricks and plaster chimney hood is still in use in this Southern European kitchen (opposite).*

*A sturdy antique table takes pride of place in this working kitchen, where the original inglenook has been used to house the stove (above).*

# KITCHEN LAYOUT

## KITCHEN PLANNING

*Storage and display shelves, eating areas and space for food preparation are all vital elements in a successful country kitchen.*

● *The kitchen, as the busiest room in the cottage, needs as much space as you can afford to give it. The conventional necessities — somewhere to store, prepare and cook food — should be arranged so that no part of the operation becomes a chore.*

● *An old-fashioned ceramic sink is not difficult to install, supported by stout brick piers which create useful storage space below. Position the sink beneath a window with a view and arrange generous and open worksurfaces, unshadowed by overhanging wall units, at either side.*

● *Old cupboards can be refaced with recycled boards to give a lived-in look to a kitchen. They provide different heights for work-surfaces made from tiles, marble, slate or wood.*

● *The country cooker which heats the house as well as the food is a welcome feature in any kitchen. Where the cooker has given way to an electric or gas replacement, a small wood-burning stove, used for warming winter soups and stews, can be a useful addition.*

# EATING AREAS

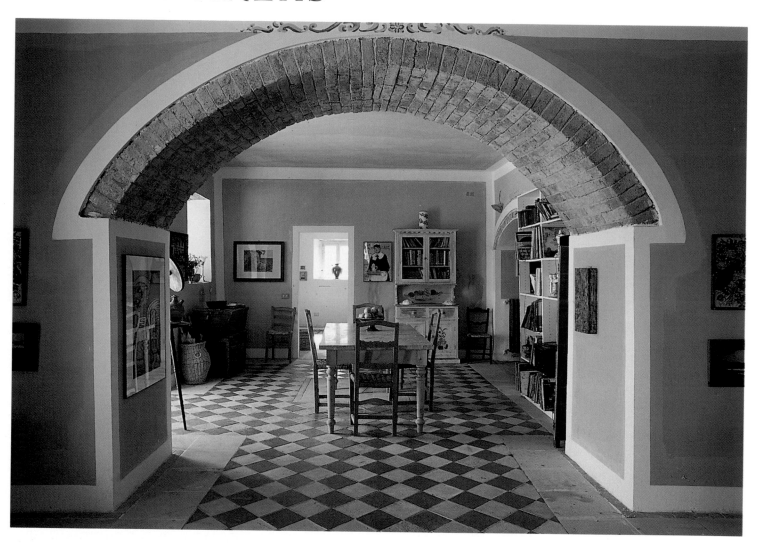

● The art of creating agreeable eating areas is adaptability. A sound surface, a serviceable chair and congenial surroundings are all that are needed.

● The fashion for allocating a room solely for formal dining has diminished, but the need to create a relaxed eating area remains. The cottage convention was to enjoy fresh food as close as possible to the cooking activities.

● A broad and spacious kitchen can be created by removing partition walls between adjoining rooms, remembering to support load-bearing walls with a beam capable of bearing the weight.

● In such surroundings table and chairs form a natural division, especially when they can be placed under a sunlit window or in a well-lit corner, surrounded by a shelf display of decorative items.

● In smaller kitchens, a drop leaf table set against a wall will suffice for everyday use. It can be pulled out into the room to seat more when the occasion demands.

● There is no necessity to slavishly collect chairs which match the table – if three ladderbacks and two Windsors feel comfortable, they will persuade diners to linger just as long as would a matching set of antique chairs.

TABLE MANNERS

The removal of a dividing wall, now supported by an elegant pale brick arch, has made a cool and calm dining area in this Umbrian farmhouse near Todi. A pink and white colour scheme diffuses the strong Italian light (above).

A collection of solid Scandinavian wooden table and chairs forms the main focal point in this simple interior (right).

AT

Social co
people s
After th
designed
dining
become
status s
    No
modes
table v
examp
cut oa
covere
chang
given
sized
peop
boar
bear
and
clear
tabl
oak
    N
bes
pot
the
sto
we
wo

R

A
i
r
v
h

# WINING AND DINING

● *The greatest benefit of living in rural surroundings is the regular opportunity to exchange indoors for outdoors. An outdoor sun trap can be made by building a south-facing stone or block and whitewash wall, and flooring the area with paving slabs or old tiles. Break up the brightness with greenery, growing an espalier fruit tree or a vine against the wall.*

● *From the Cumbrian spinning galleries to the Italian loggia, many cottages incorporated a roofed area or gallery, open to the elements, for drying produce and fleeces or storing fuel.*

● *By tiling the floors, fitting slatted roller blinds and furnishing the gallery with appropriate furniture, these areas can be transformed into outdoor rooms, ideal for entertaining.*

● *Seasoned wooden benches and chairs made from wooden slats which drain off rainwater make serviceable outdoor furniture. Given an annual coat of timber preservative, they will forgive being left out all year round. Alternatively buy a basic picnic bench with fold-down bench seats.*

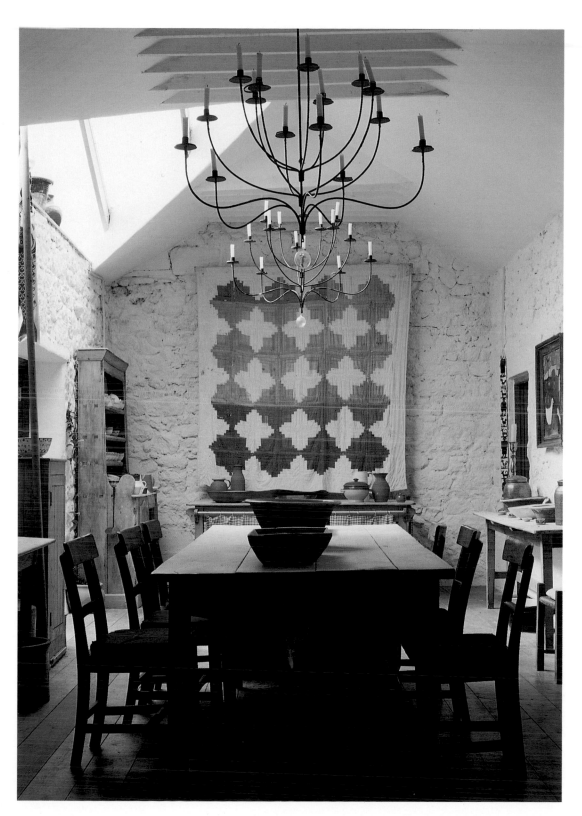

### SIMPLE STYLE

*Tempered by modern comforts, the austerity of the Shaker tradition holds this dining room in a balance between old and new (left). Simple whitewashed stone walls and the barrel ceiling provide a tranquil backdrop to the graceful candelabra and quilted wall hanging.*

### LOGGIA LIFE

*Laid for the midday meal, a round table hides beneath a checkered table cloth (opposite above). Plain wooden chairs meet the needs of the diners who can enjoy their food beside a pretty paved area of the garden.*

### COOL TILES

*A combination of timber, tiles and wrought iron furnish a relaxed dining area. Muslin drapes can be dropped across the windows to shield the diners from fierce sunlight, while the old cast-iron oven can still be lit with logs on a winter's night (opposite below).*

# LIVING ROOMS

The living room does not have a long history since most cottages possessed no other living room than the kitchen. And yet most small country houses have one these days, so where did it come from?

If, during an informal cottage dinner party, some obtuse time machine were to reverse the clock by a century or so, guest and host would probably find themselves face to face with a benign cow chewing the cud and a roost of hens clucking in annoyance. The pretty hand-blocked wallpaper would be replaced by several coats of flaking whitewash, the deep, scroll-armed sofa by a single three-legged stool and the rich, walnut corner cupboard by a hay-filled stall. While kitchens have tended to stay in the same place, living rooms have been converted from what once would have housed the cottager's animals.

Most families were content with a large kitchen and an attic bedroom, provided the precious house cow and hens were under cover and close to hand. Until the nineteenth century, and in some parts of Europe until well into the twentieth century, the cottager either stalled their livestock on the ground floor and lived above them, benefitting from the heat of the animals below, or else placed them at one end of the longhouse.

In Britain, the animals were being evicted to outside quarters from the nineteenth century on, as the commemorative datestones over many a stable and cowshed show. Faced with a new room to fit and furnish, the cottager had no option other than to follow the fashion for creating a drawing room or parlour.

Following the fashion of their better-off neighbours, as keenly as those neighbours would eventually copy their own cottage interiors, the parlour became the best room, furnished like a Victorian melodrama with dark drapes, an upright piano and a dark-stained dado below a cheap printed wallpaper. It was a place where children might play if they did so quietly and where the dead might lie before burial.

Such sombre surroundings did not last long in the cottage. The householder needed space for the burgeoning number of redundant articles from other parts of the house, and eclectic collections of old heating irons, butter pats, wooden decoys, china honey pots and tin animals nestled against those two items new to most cottages, wireless sets and book shelves.

Ironically, this was taking place as the style setters were hastily adopting the ideas of the Arts and Crafts movement, looking to juxtapose natural materials and textures with simple country furniture and solid-looking fireplaces.

Nowadays, cottage living rooms are often more spacious as a result of knocking down interior walls and combining two or three original rooms. In addition to storing and displaying collections, the atmosphere in a living room can be completely transformed by its furniture and soft furnishings. Floral fabrics create a traditional room, while uphostered chairs and sofas in plain fabrics make for a more formal drawing room. For simple sophistication, try combining checks and stripes in colours such as cool blue, yellow and terracotta.

Let the building itself guide you in your choice of decoration. While the clean lines of a Corbusier chair or an Art Deco table may look at home in the city, a cottage living room will be more comfortable if furnished with a traditional wooden rocking chair or a voluminous loose-covered armchair. Modern elements can be successful in an old building however, if used sparingly among older pieces.

BARED BEAMS

*Usually concealed beneath plasterboard ceilings, the crafted complexity of this roof construction has been left exposed. Broad windows and wide doors prevent a top-heavy feel to the room.*

# COLOUR TREATMENTS

● Light plays tricks with colour. Before committing a strong colour to an expanse of wall or ceiling, try a sample first on an area which will receive both artificial interior light and natural daylight.

● Old cottage wall surfaces (above), can vary from fresh plaster and brick to timber lintels and beams. Prepare surfaces like

these by sanding down and priming fresh wood, repairing broken or crumbling plaster with cellulose filler, sanded smooth when dry, and by priming fresh plaster with a neutral emulsion paint, well watered down.

● Fashion is fickle with paint finishes, insisting on a particular finish one season and advocating

the opposite view twelve months later. In reality, there is nothing new under the sun, only a kaleidoscope of colour schemes to be re-invented again and again.

● The addition of a trompe-l'oeil painting to raw or coloured plaster is an effective way of introducing colour, pattern and texture to a plain wall.

● This soft pink interior (right) has retained the traditional plaster finish on its gable wall, referring back to the days when, every spring, the cottage was given a fresh coat of whitewash inside and out in order to bear the next year's worth of stormy weather and sunshine.

# FIREPLACES AND STOVES

The living room fireplace has been the central focus of the room from the time when a fire was no more than a pile of smouldering twigs and dried cow dung, to the smart modern substitute of a look-a-like, gas-powered log fire.

The original cottage fireplace, set centre stage in the middle of the room, was surrounded by low stools and benches, the ground-level seating arrangments made necessary by the smoke-filled rooms.

During the affluent English Elizabethan period, the start of what became known as the Great Rebuilding in Britain, fireplaces and hearths were built into walls. Positioning a fireplace in the centre of the old cottage, the chimney rearing up through the roof, divided the house into two distinct parts for the first time.

Although the rest of the house might be made of stone or timber, the chimney and fireplace was usually formed from brick. Used for cooking purposes, the fireplace was a cavernous affair with room for pots and pans hung from chains over the glowing embers. Some put a pine fire surround with a high mantelpiece above and set an earthenware bread oven or a chamber for smoking fish or meat into the side of the fireplace. Others favoured a broad lintel or bressumer, often of fire-resistant elm, to hold the chimney in place. A short skirt or curtain hung from the lintel to keep back the fire smoke. Beneath it an iron firedog or a log basket kept the blazing wood at bay while an iron fireback protected the back wall and radiated heat into the room. Firebacks were often heavily decorated – a favourite design was made by pressing pieces of rope and simple wood-carved designs into a sand mould before pouring the molten metal over the top.

In summer, the fireplace was filled with a decoration of dried flowers or pine cones or, especially in North America, covered with hand-painted fire boards which plugged the draught from the chimney.

In winter, the fire was lit again and kept alight until spring, although many a northern farmer claimed to have kept the house fire alight for a century or so.

The use of fossil fuels lead to a new technology of fireboxes, raised hearths, grates and stoves, many of which were installed more for their good looks than for their efficiency. But in the cold north, the wood burning cast-iron or earthenware stove reigned supreme. The tall Scandinavian ceramic stoves, which heated stones stored in a tiled chamber over the fire, radiated warmth like night storage heaters, while the 'American' stove, which appeared in Pennsylvania in the early 1700s, drew in cold air from outside and breathed it into the living room.

Although central heating systems finally swept away the need for a central hearth, the open log fire and the wood stove have survived, providing the main focus for many a cottage living room. There are now myriad variations in the form of wood-burning stoves, simple wood surrounds, floral tiles or dramatic stone mantels.

### UNREPENTANT LUXURY

*The cushioned comfort of a chintz-covered sofa and chairs is enhanced by a blazing log fire (opposite below left). The log basket, fire bellows and dramatic candlestand hark back to the past and add a cosy ambience to enhance this meditative and comfortable living room.*

### COTTAGE INGLENOOK

*When fireplaces like these (opposite above) were first built into the English country cottage, firewood was cheap and plentiful. Now, diminishing supplies emphasize the practicality of a more modest multi-fuel stove which, as the centrepiece of a cavernous stone inglenook, can become a feature in its own right.*

### FIRES WITHOUT FIREPLACES

*Although it needs a chimney, the firebox and flue of a wood stove requires no fireplace (opposite below right). Such fires, set on a fireproof plinth of old bricks or tiles, create a heart-warming feature in any traditional cottage living room.*

# COUNTRY FURNITURE

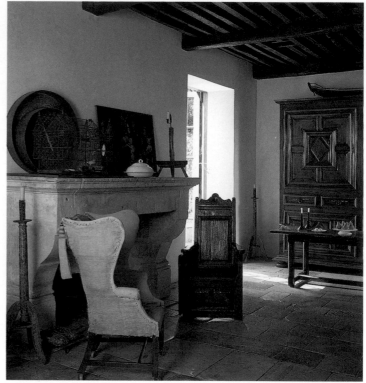

The age of plastic, not to mention steel and nylon, has equipped us with the basic necessities of life, but the appeal of natural materials runs deep. Outside a museum of old buildings it would be difficult to find a dwelling furnished with nothing more than items made from wood, rush, reed and clay. And yet a century ago, the average cottager had no other alternative. It was a dependency that made him or her extraordinarily inventive.

The sparse furniture in a Hebridean cottage at the turn of this century might have run to a chest, some stools or logs for seats and, hung upon the wall, two or three wooden boards used as individual lap tables at meal times. The original family chests, sometimes carved out of a solid tree trunk, had one inherent disadvantage; the flat surface of the lid could not be used if the owner needed to be constantly rummaging around inside the chest. The court cupboard with open shelves over the closed storage space below overcame the problem. Tall enough to act as a room partition and frequently too large to be removed from the house without

being dismantled, the seventeenth-century householder began to enclose the upper shelves to create the press-cupboard. Three hundred years later, country people in parts of Ireland still refer to their cupboards as presses.

Traditional furniture was made according to the customs of each region, but the ubiquitous dresser conquered all conservatism and was adopted right across the Northern world. Made of whatever materials were locally available, from Scandinavian pine to English oak, the dressers displayed bowls and cups, just as they do today.

The settle, the forerunner of the modern sofa was similarly constructed of local wood, from ash, elm and birch to fruitwood, pine and deal. Here vernacular design resulted in a wide variety of styles including the 'seize' which looked more like an open-backed park bench, and the settle-bed.

## MADE TO MEASURE

*Most country cottages were once sparsely furnished and pride of place was given to a single fine piece of furniture.*

# DECORATED·FURNITURE

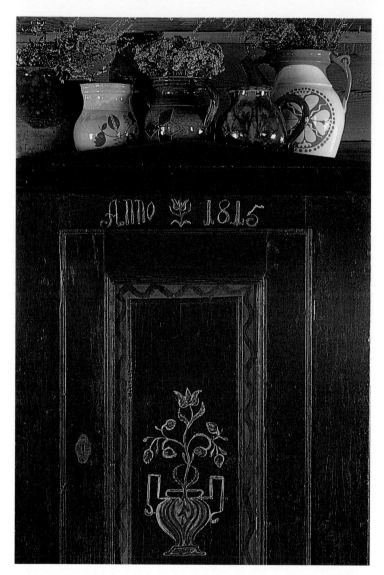

rarely developed in isolation. In the same way that the Iberian peninsular enjoys a Moorish influence, the Rococo and neo-Classical styles of France played a part in shaping the interiors of Scandinavian houses. Retained in rural homes long after the aristocracy had adopted new fashions, the spirited style of the traditional Scandinavian interior was imported to New England by the American settlers.

The abundant supplies of softwoods in both these countries were used to build the cottage and make its furniture. Paint, its pigments drawn from natural materials, provided protection and decoration.

Since the family bible was the only book liable to be found in most peasant homes, visual references for the furniture painter were limited to the natural surroundings. Itinerant painters were inclined to introduce fresh ideas into the remote settlements they visited, but the decorative tradition remained firmly rooted in folk art.

The art of stencilling which reached Europe from the Far East and Asia was also adopted by folk artists and both stencilling and painting furniture have enjoyed a revival.

Simple stencils, cut from acetate sheeting or oiled stencil boards can be used to add colour to an otherwise featureless wall. On emulsioned wall surfaces, acrylics, poster paints or emulsion paints themselves work well.

Experiment with different paints on furniture; emulsions and diluted acrylics can be used with a protective top coat of tinted varnish. Prepare surfaces with as much diligence as you can muster and use a solid primer to seal the surface and key the decorative coats.

## PAINTED DISPLAY

*The habit of stripping pine furniture has made painted wall cupboards like these (left) comparatively rare until recently. This simply painted cupboard is enhanced by a display of bright glazed jugs.*

## SCANDINAVIAN BLUES

*A blue-tiled corner stove (right) warms a room furnished with painted pieces. The manufacture of a longcase or a grandfather clock like this one standing on a decorated chest, was a traditional cottage industry.*

The provincial fondness for colour, stronger in southern Europe than Britain, lead to a rich variety of painted furniture. In France, where graffitti artists still use stencils to make their mark, the *dominotiers* produced small painted papers or 'dominoes' bought by the boxful at the market and used as friezes on furniture. In America, journeymen artists roved amongst the East Coast settlers, overlaying bright pictures of birds and beehives, fruits and flowers on any and every surface, from the backs of rocking chairs and wooden cupboards to the living-room floorboards.

Vernacular styles, although unique to their own region,

# COUNTRY SOFT FURNISHINGS

Traditional cottagers were no less fond of their creature comforts than we are today; they simply worked harder and longer to acquire them. The Shaker societies, for example, who pioneered the silk industry in Kentucky, raised their own silk worms, picked the cocoons, which yielded a mere pound of silk to a whole bushel of cocoons, and reeled, dyed and then wove the cloth themselves.

While most of the cottagers' soft furnishings were made for sale and a small profit, some at least remained in the home. Upholstered furniture might have been beyond the purse of the average cottager, but the product of the 'quishion loome' was not. These hay-filled cushions softened the impact of hard wooden country seats in the same way as foam box cushions and bolsters adorn window seats today, while linen drapes, embroidered wall hangings and lace curtains, each according to the local style, were also found in country homes.

Before the Industrial Revolution, the very materials for soft furnishings came from the garden and beyond. Irish linen rose from fields of white flax and Welsh wool from the sheep grazing beside the blackberries, elderberries and cow parsley that were used to dye their fleeces.

Thankfully, contemporary soft furnishings involve nothing more labour-intensive than choosing a fabric, although the plethora of fabrics and designs on the market now make choosing colours and themes a daunting task if you are starting from scratch.

Furniture and architectural features are not the only medium for soft furnishings in the living room. Large baskets, traditionally used for storing logs, may be embellished with simple gingham fabric, loosely sewn around their top edge and tied in an informal knot. A perfect home for children's toys or untidy newspapers and magazines.

## DEEP-SEATED COMFORT

*The formal panelling of this small living room is softened by a deep and comfortable sofa filled with delicately decorated cushions.*

# COUNTRY CRAFTS AND TEXTILES

Following on from the nineteenth-century factory boom which not only swept away cottage crafts, but removed the craftspeople themselves from the country to the towns, there has been a steady revival in recent years of rural, handmade articles as carpet makers, iron masters, glass blowers, clock makers, potters, weavers and clog makers move out of town once more to set up country businesses.

Whether the view from the cottage window was a Mediterranean olive grove or the heathered hillsides of a Yorkshire moor, the old country house invariably contained some example of the cottage crafts. There were precious few ornaments to be had apart from what the cottagers made themselves. Many items were utilitarian – painted tin coffee pots, copper warming pans, cane carpet beaters and decorated herb choppers. Other items were kept for their spiritual insurance value. Horse brasses were hung from the mare's harness to ward off the evil eye, while corn dollies, plaited from the last sheaf of the harvest and felled by the reapers' thrown sickles, were displayed to ensure a good harvest in the year ahead.

In the Finnish province of Karelia where the landworkers lived together in their timbered farmhouses, anyone entering the living room bowed first to the religous icon set in the corner and then to the pagan horse's head set by the hearth. They also used the horse's head as a device for sorting yarn.

Carpets and rugs were traditionally made, if not by the householder themselves, then by some local craftsperson whose fees were judged to be lower than their talents. Not that carpets appeared in many cottages before the late nineteenth century. The present abundance of both carpets and rugs on the floors of the contemporary cottage is a new phenomenon. Two centuries ago, carpets covered tables, rugs covered beds and floor cloths covered floors.

The floor cloth was a piece of canvas or oil cloth often painted to mimic the knots of floor boards or the pattern of floor tiles, like the linoleum floor coverings which replaced them in the mid nineteenth century. In the Americas too, carpets were a rarity and bare, varnished or simply painted floorboards the rule. When, in the late nineteenth century, the Shakers started to relax their attitude towards ornamentation, they began to manufacture rugs and knitted carpets.

Straw, cane and rush mats were more common in the south, while rugs were prevalent in the north. One thickly textured version involved weaving strips of coloured rag tied together through a strong warp of woollen yarn. The hooked rug which probably originated in Scandinavia (rug comes from the Swedish *rugg* or rough hair) was variously known as a clootie or stobbie in northern Britain. The clootie was made by looping strips of rag through a coarse canvas backing or a redundant potato sack.

WARM CURTAINS

*Handmade textiles created from locally available materials would once have been the only form of soft furnishings in a country cottage. Ornamentation did not become an integral part of the cottage interior until the late nineteenth century.*

# DISPLAYS

The contemporary cottage living room would not be complete without its fair share of collected treasures, whether they be painted ceramics displayed neatly on a set of wooden shelves, copper pans suspended from oak beams or watercolour paintings hung on walls.

Colour plays an important role in any display, so think about the backdrop before embarking on any painting or decorating. Vivid blue-painted shelves against a mint green wall for example, could make for a distracting mix.

Where possible, make full use of any existing nooks and crannies in the room for display. Redundant serving hatches, stone window recesses and generous sills all have potential as display areas for prized possessions.

Other means of displaying objects include traditional dressers, which can be used for storage too, built-in alcove shelves and cupboards and, of course, mantlepieces and inglenook fireplaces.

*Built-in cupboards and shelves were regularly incorporated into country homes to serve as herb shelves, salt boxes and food stores (right). The alcove on this English cottage wall has been turned into a trompe-l'oeil with an arched hood and a pair of painted shutters (above).*

Chapter Four

# SLEEPING QUARTERS

*Sloping rafters, low ceilings and an economical use of limited roof space create country cottage bedrooms which are warm, snug and simple. Cottage bedrooms often occupy the loft area, where the morning light once lit upon stores of fruit and grain spread across the attic floorboards. When, in the nineteenth century, the cottager began to copy the example of his more affluent farmer neighbours and converted this storage space into bedrooms, boxbeds and settles gave way to cast iron and brass beds, which called for an increased sense of comfort, while cotton counterpanes and colourful quilts replaced sheepskins and furs. Popular taste led to the introduction of wooden washstands and china water jugs, bedside rugs and floral curtains.*

*If the provision of separate bedrooms was late in coming to the old cottage, the arrival of the bathroom was even later, but these days the cottage mood has extended into both the bedroom and bathroom. Rarely grand and seldom lavish, country bedrooms and bathrooms should be, above all else, modest, cheerful and cosy.*

SOUND SLEEPING

*The muted pink plaster paint finish of this Scandinavian bedroom is enhanced by delightful trompe-l'oeil of garden flowers and a painted swag at picture rail height. Bleached floorboards blend effortlessly with the rough-painted chair and side table.*

# BEDROOMS

The medieval habit of sleeping by the fireside was still widespread in Europe a hundred years ago. Bedcupboards, settle beds and even a plain slab of stone set into the side wall of the kitchen, served the sleepers, but once the cottager decided that sleeping in the kitchen would no longer do, different bedrooms were made to suit different cottages.

Those reluctant to leave the warmth of the main room built a bedroom annexe directly off the kitchen, scarcely bigger than the family bed itself. Common in North America and Northern Ireland, the annexe was often insulated with a ceiling of woven grass or rush matting and later with old newspapers pasted across the ceiling and concealed beneath a coat of whitewash.

Building bedrooms upstairs depended on the shape of the cottage roof. On bare, windswept heaths and open, coastal plains, the cottage kept its head down low and roof space was minimal. In the kinder lowlands, where there was a good living to be made from the land, the two-storey cottage was commonplace.

In highland areas where long winters and deep snowfalls were customary, roofs were sharp pitched and steep, allowing for a warren of upper-floor rooms to be slipped easily into the roof space.

In larger cottages, a stone staircase wound up around the back of the hearth to reach the loft above, or was inserted as a steep flight of wooden steps leading straight up from the kitchen into the loft space. Lit by a pair of tiny dormer windows at floor level, the loft could be divided into a balcony bedroom which lead on to a second, enclosed room. Sharing space with the stores of apples, fleeces or grain, the best bed would be stood over the heated kitchen below. One typical version was to have a divan built above the warm charnel, a raised recess in the kitchen ceiling used to hang bacon and herbs.

Some cottages, like the Welsh *croglofft*, were too small even for a stairway. (Being a land of small houses, the Welsh language contains as many different words for a small house as the Eskimos have names for snow). The *croglofft* possessed two ground-floor rooms, a kitchen open to the rafters and a parlour, with a bedroom squeezed in over the parlour. Again, a straw or rush woven ceiling insulated the little bedroom and a loft ladder, rather than a staircase, lead up to the bed.

Cottage bedrooms today should encourage rest and relaxation, be neither too chintzy nor too strident in their decoration, and reflect the traditional country elements of decoration – soft colours combined with a variety of natural textures and materials.

Here, as elsewhere in the home, hand-crafted rugs, furniture and fabrics would once have been the only form of embellishment and storage, so think about traditional forms of decoration when planning your bedroom scheme. Individual chests of drawers and wardrobes are preferable to built-in units in the country bedroom, as are individual beds rather than mass-produced divans. Keep fabrics simply floral or subtly checked, and consider your requirements for privacy or light at the windows. Delicate lace or muslin drapes look entirely at home in the country bedroom, but remember to think about whether you need to keep out noise or bright sunlight before consigning your thicker curtains to the obscurity of the blanket box.

LYING IN LUXURY

*The grandeur of this four poster bed draped with white curtains is matched only by the direct view of the garden from the bedroom door. A generous lace-like curtain affords the room some privacy.*

# BEDROOM LAYOUT

*Restrained simplicity and the use of traditional furniture and furnishings have turned this spare bedroom (left above) into a welcome retreat. From the local quilt and rag rug to the blanket chest, wooden bed and ledge-and-brace door, the basic elements combine to recreate a cosy and straightforward country style based on natural materials.*

*Use of light is important, especially in country surroundings where natural daylight is usually in abundance. On one side of a building, windows will open onto muted sunsets; on the other, to the clear light of dawn. By taking over a corner room with windows on two sides, this bedroom (left below) catches the late evening light and gives a bright start to the day, while the tiled stove set against one wall is guaranteed to take the chill off the morning air. Pleasantly spacious rooms like these can double as living or work rooms.*

A glimpse into the sleeping quarters of the average country cottage a century ago would reveal a tiny room tucked in under the eaves of the house. Nowadays, bedrooms are often rooms that have been converted from former living areas.

Here two ground-floor bedrooms exhibit on the one hand a cool and elegant decorative scheme and, on the other, a congenially snug option: a pair of black iron bedsteads (above left) stand on terracotta tiles in a calm, cream room. On cold nights the fire in this former living room can be lit to add a touch of luxury.

Similarly (left below) the imposing fireplace in this former kitchen has been retained and now forms the central focus of the room. The stable door which opens directly onto the garden, the cottage washstand and the handy fireside cupboard express a delightfully traditional cottage feel.

# BEDS

The current expectation that we spend a third of our life in our beds did not hold true in the past when the working day began at dawn or sooner. Nevertheless the cottager expected to sleep in some comfort.

Social division kept the impoverished in their place, but the demand for servants gave the less affluent an insight into the sleeping habits of the wealthy. Seeing that the rich slept on feather or combed wool mattresses, cocooned in their curtained four-poster beds, the poor were less inclined to hold fast to their traditional straw mattresses and old-fashioned bed cupboards.

An aspiring yeoman farmer might install a passable reproduction of an Elizabethan four-poster complete with drapes and curtains. The headboard sometimes contained a small cupboard and there would certainly be an additional ledge or shelf on which to stand the candle or rushlight, with its attendant fire risks.

But in the small country cottage space was at a premium. A truckle bed, like a low divan on wheels, could be stored during the day beneath the main bed. Then there was the press bedstead, which folded up to resemble a chest of drawers, and the more useful settle bed, popular in North America and Ireland which, like the sofa bed, folded into a seat or low sideboard. Another portable bed was the rope bunk, made by stringing cords between the headboard and footboard and tightening them against a bedboard at night.

The Breton and Scandinavian box- or cupboard-bed was economic with both heat and space. Often made with the children's bunk above the parental bed, the front and sides were decorated with painted wooden panels while woollen hangings on curtain rails could be closed during the night to keep in the warmth. Others, built into the cottage wall beside the hearth, were closed off in the day by a pair of panelled doors which formed the back of the fireside settle.

In warmer climates the cottagers slept on half-headed or stump beds, with a plain headboard at the top end. The mattress was laid across a web of rush or rope straps, with a rush or canvas mat between the webbing and the mattress. Gradually, the forged iron bedstead, already in use in Italy, and the brass bedstead, with springs replacing the old webbing, gravitated down through the social classes in the eighteenth and nineteenth centuries.

The most expensive traditional mattresses were filled with swan's down, while the cottager's economy version would be filled with heather, animal hair and even beech leaves. Additional mattresses were used for extra comfort – in the seventeeth century Cardinal Wolsey expected to find no less than eight beneath him. While textile crafts remained a cottage industry, good linen and blankets or fleeces covered the beds, together with the traditional bedcover and the handcrafted patchwork quilt, which added a bold dash of decorative colour and texture to the cottage bedroom.

BOX BEDS

*This fine example of a box bed has a sleeping space behind the curtains as well as a bunk bed above. Once common throughout Scandinavia, northern France and Britain, the box bed can still provide serviceable sleeping arrangements for young children.*

# BEDS AND BEDDING

● *A good bed will not last forever, but given a good mattress and a sympathetic choice of bedlinen, the traditional beds shown here are as comfortable as they are good-looking. This American wooden bed (left), with its dramatically tall turned posts and deep mattress, is covered with a traditional quilt.*

● *Large family beds were seldom found in smaller country cottages, but settle beds such as this green painted example from Finland (below far left) provided the ideal solution. By day they were used as a bench seat and by night, with a straw, heather or combed wool mattress, they served the sleeper well enough.*

● *Metal bedsteads (below left) became a classic country cottage design, only to be abandoned in the early twentieth century. Many have been exhumed from the bottom of the garden to be fully restored with a gleaming new coat of paint.*

● *This iron bedstead (right above) has been finished off with an elevated lace-edged valance to complement the white bedcover. Light lace bedding (below right) provides an effective contrast to a carved bedhead in dark wood. Another traditional bed, the north European cot, (below far right) is enhanced with fretwork carvings at the head and feet.*

# BEDROOM FABRICS

BEDROOM FABRICS

*Soft furnishings in the country bedroom should be uncomplicated. Try using natural fabrics in a combination of simple colours and patterns and such as cool lemon and blue checks and ginghams or gentle florals on a white ground.*

*Curtains look more homely if they are full length, adding a sense of luxury to simple surroundings.*

*Bedcovers and bedlinen should blend or contrast with your chosen decorative scheme, while cushions, bolsters and throws can lend extra colour interest to large beds.*

*On this lightweight version of the traditional tester, or four-poster bed (left), white sheer curtains enclose the bed at night. A deep valance and a fabric skirt over the bedside table complement the bed curtains.*

*A white bed drape edged with pink bobble trim (below left) defines the bed space against the pink wall of this rural bedroom. Similarly (below right) a bed is framed by deep white lace drapes hung from the ceiling above a narrow bed embellished with carved bedheads. These show off the fabric to good effect.*

*An American field bed (opposite) complete with a delicate arched tester draped with a netted coverlet takes pride of place in this simply defined bedroom.*

The ideal bathroom as defined by one architect is a room where you can feel comfortable when naked; if the bathroom fails to conform to this description, remodel it or remove it to a warmer, lighter situation.

If you have inherited a miniature bathroom, look for space-saving ideas; could the bath be re-sited in a roomy bedroom and a shower set in its place? Would a mirrored wall impart a lighter, more airy feel to the room? Could a sunken bath and shower, set against the far wall, solve the problem?

Opt for warming effects in a chilly, oversized bathroom: a cushioned floor, an old-fashioned cast iron radiator painted red, luxurious velvet curtains and a sympathetic colour finish. Replace white tiles with hot Mediterranean glazes or paint over the old tiles with a coat of eggshell yacht paint, followed by a warm gloss.

Replace the old bath with a more modest-sized substitute, projecting it into the room rather than parking it conventionally along one wall. Use tongue-and-groove panelling up to waist height, painted to match the walls. Introduce a dressing table and a pair of coloured rattan chairs and bring back wooden venetian blinds, which let in light yet maintain a sense of privacy.

A spacious bathroom can take a large and luxurious bath, free-standing on its claw feet, but a smaller three-quarter length bath, which is more economical with water, can be just as effective boxed-in with recycled mahogany floorboards.

As with any other room, it is the fine details which give a sense of character. Cane baskets and candles, green plants and driftwood, seashells and sailing boats – let your imagination run riot.

TILE STYLE

*A beautifully bizarre collection of tiles creates a spirited pattern on this bathroom wall. The painted bath, set out into the room, takes full advantage of available space, while the carpet adds a touch of luxury.*

# Chapter Five

# THE
# COTTAGE
# GARDEN

*A good cottage garden should amount to more than the sum of its parts. It may include a shrub-fringed lawn, a path edged with flowers or a productive vegetable plot, but its totality goes beyond the purely horticultural. The asparagus bed will feed the body and the bougain-villea in flower will feed the eye, but the garden as a whole also has the power to feed the soul.*

*From its modest origins as a randomly planted plot of vegetables and its over abundance of easily cultivated, low-maintenance flowers such as roses, hollyhocks and honeysuckle, the contemporary cottage garden often boasts an amalgamation of traditional formality and freeform planting. By mixing a formal layout of herbs, for example, with areas of haphazard planting, such a garden can combine the restrained with the untrained to create separate 'rooms' of colour, texture and atmosphere that are both useful and decorative.*

## DISCREET ORDER

*In the apparent chaos of the country garden, discreet order reigns. Amongst the profusion of foxgloves, sweet williams, poppies, mallow and cornflowers lining the gravel path, each plant has its allotted place. Many of these classic flowers were once grown specifically for culinary or medicinal uses.*

# LOCAL LANDSCAPES

Early cottage gardens were practical, productive units, their plants grown as much for medicinal and superstitious reasons as for culinary purposes – lavender repelled fleas and bistort kept away disease, while house leeks protected against lightning and a rowan tree was a defence against witchcraft.

The spirit of recycling thrived as plants were propagated and seeds were collected and saved. There was a healthy exchange of plants between gardeners who worked for the grand country houses and their more modest neighbours in the village. But, unlike the manor or château gardens with their contrived landscapes and formal designs, the cottage garden had no set planting pattern; plants grew in profusion but with a purpose. Herbs were especially popular country plants, being both useful and decorative: scented hyssop was strewn across the cottage floor; angelica and rosemary seed, after cooking over a slow heat, perfumed the house, and lemon balm was used to polish and scent oak furniture.

In the Mediterranean lowlands, many gardens remain as they were several centuries ago. Devoted to fruit and vegetable cultivation and the rearing of livestock, the Mediterranean cottager practised a sustaining rotation of grazing and fallow land which enriched the soil and established a healthy ecological balance. The fallow land, freckled with flowering meadow herbs served as a lawn; an intensively cultivated kitchen garden supplied the household with fresh vegetables; while sheep and hens kept down the grass in the orchard.

In Britain especially, the cottage gardener gradually began to grow plants for their good looks alone. By the early 1900s, the traditional cottage grounds, with their profusion of hollyhocks and roses and neat rows of onions and peas, became a recognizable pattern, repeated all over the country, providing inspiration for international garden designers.

In time, a two-way exchange of ideas resulted in the cottage garden being influenced by grander gardens. Features of formal gardens such as the hedged kitchen garden, the leisurely sward, the rose-bowered pergola and topiared trees have been scaled-down and incorporated into the cottage garden. No longer confined to densely packed, informal flower borders, the small garden can these days incorporate a range of landscapes in miniature – woodland and water gardens, rock and rose gardens, *parterre* and parkland – without losing its integrity.

The making of a good garden requires only time and hard work and the rewards are immeasurable. Even if householders hard-pressed for time do no more than keep the weeds at bay and import the occasional tray of geraniums from the village market each spring, they will still find themselves working with nature and enjoying it. The rural landscape is a patchwork quilt of fields, woods, heaths and hillsides stitched together by handmade boundaries of hedges, ditches and stonewalls. The last half century has transformed it almost beyond recognition. Altered to make the business of farming more efficient, small fields have been merged into prairie-sized units, moorlands have been ditched, drained and put to the plough, and woodlands felled and turned to grazing land. The changes, instituted to reduce the labour force and mechanize the farming process, have had a more radical effect on the look of the land than anything which has occured in the past two hundred years.

For much the same reasons, cottage gardens mirrored the new age. In the early post-war years, garden design books advocated layouts which were easy to maintain, neat and dull. The labour-intensive vegetable plot was put down to grass, orchards were rationalized to make way for the riding mower, and flower beds were shrunk to manageable sizes.

But the charm of the countryside lies in its variety; secretive lanes threading their way past hedgerowed meadows, old tracks meandering through ancient but productive woods, a stone packhorse bridge crossing an unkempt stream. Saddened by this loss of local diversity and spurred on by the spirit of conservation, many cottage gardeners have begun to recreate the variety of the countryside at home.

### FLOURISHING BLOSSOMS

*Wreathed in the towering tendrils of a climbing shrub, this small house looks out on a fertile garden in full bloom. Additional flowers are planted in stone troughs stood on old saddle stones.*

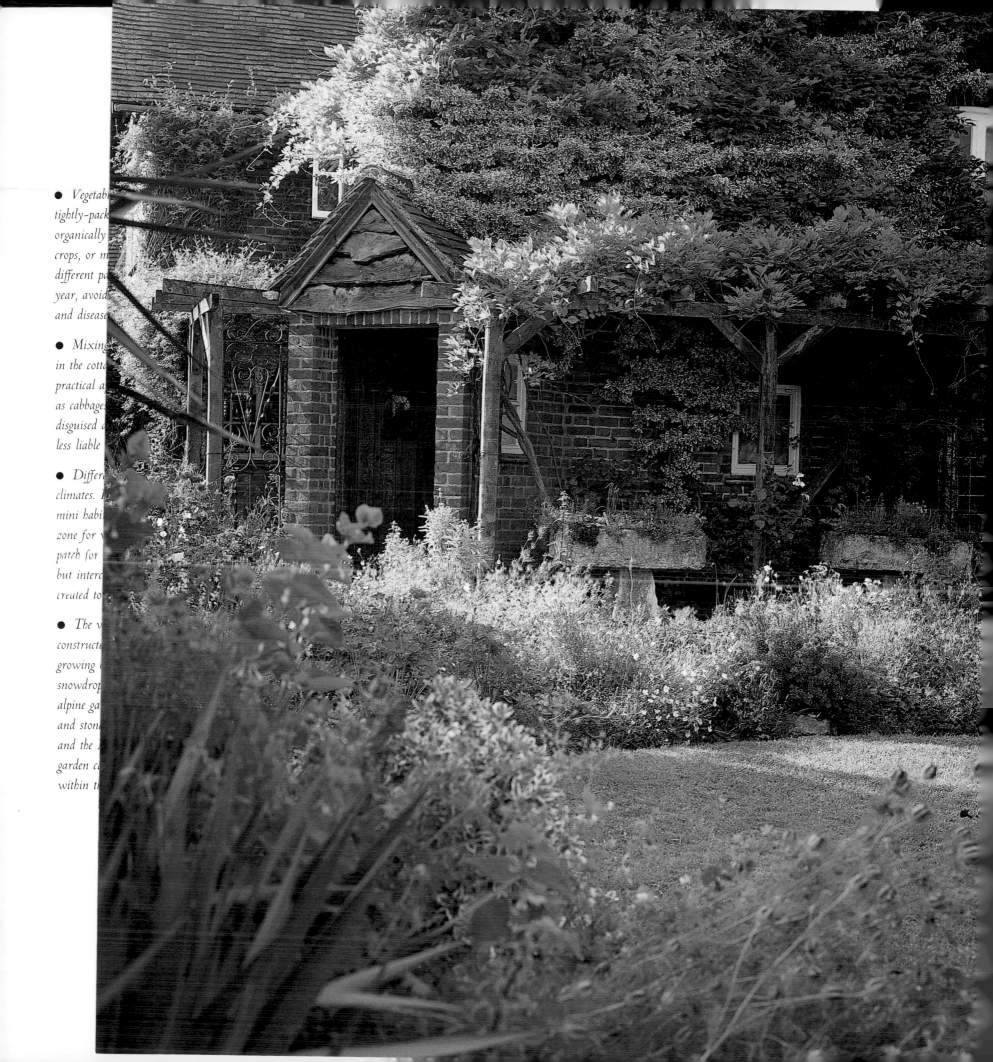

● Vegetab_
tightly-pack_
organically _
crops, or m_
different pa_
year, avoid_
and disease_

● Mixing _
in the cott_
practical a_
as cabbage_
disguised a_
less liable _

● Differe_
climates. I_
mini habi_
zone for _
patch for _
but interc_
created to _

● The v_
constructe_
growing _
snowdrop_
alpine ga_
and ston_
and the _
garden c_
within t_

### PLANTING

*Grown for their soaring spikes of flowers which produce a wall of blossom in summer and early autumn, hollyhocks thrive in a well drained soil and full sun. Appropriately associated with country gardens, the hollyhock had already found its way into cottage gardens by the fifteenth century; it was among those listed in a poem penned by John the Gardener in 1440, along with plants like foxgloves, roses, lavender, cowslip and catmint.*

*Then as now, such flowers flourish in a well-fed and nourished soil. Forked over and cleared of weeds in the winter, flower borders need a rich top dressing of compost or well-rotted manure before the plants begin their spring growth.*

*In an established garden, plants need to be thinned out and divided to avoid overcrowding. In a new garden, plants bought from the nursery, or passed on by a benevolent neighbour, are planted with an eye on their final height and mass; hollyhocks, which may need to be staked, are best grown against a sunny wall at the back of the flower bed to create a backdrop for intermediate and low growing plants.*

# STRUCTURES AND DIVIDERS

Ever since people-pressure sent settlers to the far corners of the globe, the cottage gardener has been keen to adopt the best of the plant hunters' finds. The chrysanthemum, which arrived in Holland from China in 1689, was firmly established in small gardens by the nineteenth century, while tulips brought from Constantinople in 1554 became valued collectors' items in the seventeenth century, only to become commonplace in lowland Europe a century later. Tobacco, sunflowers and that monarch of vegetables, the potato, were brought to Europe from the New World and rapidly utilized by the cottager gardener.

Garden features and dividers were also taken from one country to another. Holly, box, yew and other evergreen hedges, pergolas dripping with roses, wisteria-hung trellises, dry stone walls and larch-lap fences all crossed national frontiers as garden fashion demanded.

However, the cottage gardener was less concerned with keeping up appearances than with keeping animals in or out. The cottager who allowed his prize ram to stray from grazing his orchard and sample his neighbour's bean patch could spark off a lifelong feud, and the Danish expression that 'good fences make good neighbours' was, and still is, a prudent code of conduct.

As with the stone or timber of the cottage itself, materials for fencing were gathered from the immediate surroundings. In Provence and the Pennines, stones cleared from the field were built into mellow walls which surrounded the property; in England, blackthorn saplings were planted and laid as stockproof fences – an effective hedge was one that only allowed the wind to pass through it. In North Wales and Brittany, fangs of slate waste were stood on end and wired together to create animal compounds, while in well-wooded districts thin slivers of riven ash or chestnut were turned into fence poles and runners. The thinner brushwood supported the beans and was fixed securely to cottage walls to provide a purchase for Virginia creepers, trailing roses and other climbing plants.

In much of contemporary America and southern Europe, a fence between the house and the road is considered unnecessary, even antisocial, although the natural protection of a stand of fir trees or pollarded poplars is useful to protect fruit trees or vines from unseasonable winds and rain. But where a hedgebank is part of the local landscape, it should be retained and restored wherever possible. A ragged bank of quick thorn, beech and elm which is taken out and replaced by a bare post and rail fence or a regimented line of conifers, does a disservice to both the local landscape as well as the local wildlife.

Although numerous materials are available for today's cottage gardens, from ornamental concrete blocks and galvanized wire structures to plastic framework and netting, the rural landscape still looks at its best when furnished with partitions made from natural materials. The Italian pergola, a sheltered walk which leads to some feature of the garden, and the arbor (which does not) can both be bought-in ready-made from garden centres. Pergolas may be made with treated battens set over a wood or iron frame and arbors from pre-formed wire or iron structures which are gradually cloaked beneath a plait of ivy and clematis. Natural arbors can be grown from a stand of hazel or hornbeam, their tops knitted together and the leafy framework laced with heady-scented climbers such as jasmine and honeysuckle.

ECHOING ARCHES

*Two painted arches mirror one another in a tranquil corner of New York State Garden. Combining climbing plants like clematis and roses or honeysuckle and wisteria will give a rich mix of colour and scent.*

# CONTAINERS

● *Container-grown plants make for a mobile garden: gardeners at the Palace of Versailles kept almost two million planted pots at the ready, changing displays while the Sun King dined. Pot-grown plants can extend the flower power of the smallest garden and turn the most unpromising collection of plants into an Eden.*

● *This otherwise unproductive corner (above) is ornamented with pots and barrels of flowers. Containers have their functional applications too. Pot-grown herbs can be brought inside for use in the kitchen, while an old biscuit tin buried in the herb garden will control invasive plants like mint.*

● *Where a mature tree provides difficult growing conditions at its base, red geraniums stand proudly in terracotta pots (left) to form a circle of colour.*

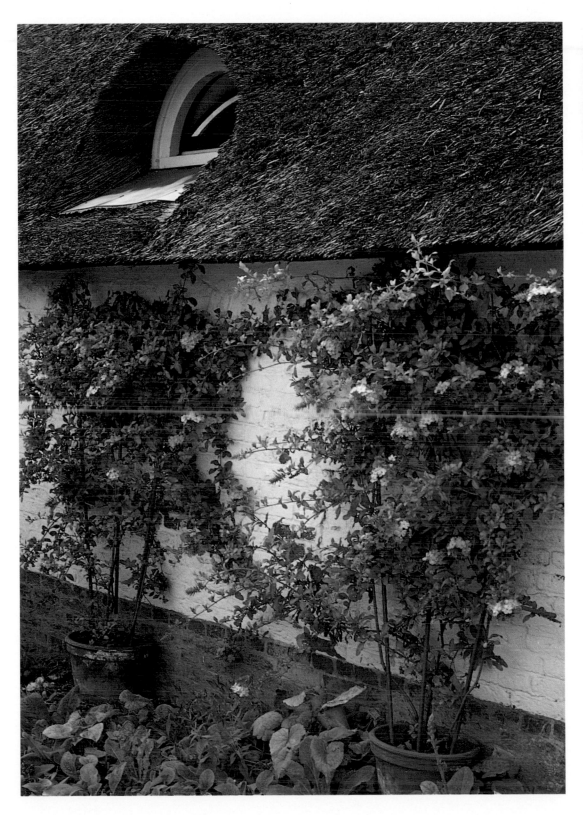

● *Frost-sensitive flowers like geraniums and begonias can be over-wintered in their containers in a cool conservatory. These ceramic flowers pots (above) are taken inside when the weather turns cool.*

● *Pot-grown shrubs (left) set against a cool north-eastern wall for the summer can be placed against a more sheltered southern wall for the winter.*

● *Anything from a formal gilded urn to a pair of old wooden clogs can be used as a plant container. What the plant requires is space to grow, good drainage and regular feeding. Ensure the base of the container has drainage holes and line it with small stones or pieces of broken pot before adding some rich compost and placing the plant inside it.*

# CONSERVATORIES

A conservatory is the one structure no-one would expect to find as part of a country cottage a century ago. Things are different today.

Many country cottagers have brought a little of the outdoors inside by adding on a conservatory. The conservatory has also found favour as an ecologically-friendly addition to a building, with a heat store in its foundations and a solar heating system in its roof.

Filled with flowering plants and pot-grown shrubs, furnished with wickerwork and protected from the noonday summer sun by white canvas blinds or breezy muslin, the conservatory emulates its grand, Victorian forefathers.

The vogue for the glazed outhouse sprang from the work of people like Decimus Burton who built the Palm House of the Royal Botanical Gardnes at Kew and the gardener Joseph Paxton, responsible for London's Crystal Palace. The Victorians used the same materials – ironwork and glass – and installed oppressive heating systems to sustain the exotic foreign plants which their relatives mailed home from far-flung corners of the Empire.

The French *serre*, a glass extension which could be used as a small sitting room, was less ambitious, and more in keeping with the modern cottage conservatory. Accompanied by a marble-topped café table and a set of metal-framed chairs, the family could sit and enjoy their evening bottle of Bordeaux surrounded by potted plants in lead-lined plant trays which lay in neat, garden-like decorative rows around the windowsill.

However, a conservatory does not suit every cottage. The southern face of a mellow old half-timbered building will not be enhanced by the addition of a great, white whale of glass and wood; the owners would do better to create a sympathetic garden house instead. Another option would be to adapt part of the house as a sun room, replacing a wall at window height with glass set in frames which harmonize with the cottage windows, or discreetly reroofing a single-storey extension with toughened roofing glass.

Conservatory or sun room, the intention is the same – to recreate the feel of *al fresco* life. Brick or quarry tiled floors, which forgive the occasional overflow of water from the shrubs and flowers, good ventilation and a sound system of shading are basic necessities. One solution to the problem of the over-heated conservatory is to plant a vine outside the building and train it inside to spread across the roof. The annual harvest of grapes which hangs ripening over your head is ample compensation for having to sweep out the annual autumnal leaf fall.

The great advantage of the modern conservatory is the added space and flexibility that it gives a home. At the same time as allowing extra light to flow into rooms which are often dark and dingy before being opened out, conservatories can either become a small room in their own right, acting as an eating area or second living room, or act as additional living space when built on to kitchens or dining rooms, for instance. Another example of their versatility is that they can act as garden 'extensions', bringing the outdoors closer when there is little true garden space on the other side of the French windows.

AL FRESCO EXISTENCE

*A family of red enamel chairs pulled up to an old timber table provides the perfect picture of life in an outdoor room. The full-grown tree provides shade and the stone arch frames a doorway into the garden.*

# REST AND RELAXATION

● *Garden furniture is now available in many different materials and colours. Choose a style which suits your particular type of garden.*

● *Elegantly proportioned wrought-iron chairs and tables fit beautifully into an eating area that is architecturally framed by a clematis- or rose-laden arbor.*

● *Chunky wooden benches treated with weatherproof preservative can sit happily in the garden throughout the year, offering a peaceful retreat from gardening chores.*

● *In a small garden, furnish a seating area with foldaway tables and chairs. Try collecting several wooden chairs, each painted a different colour, for an interesting and variable effect.*

● *If there is space at the bottom of the garden you can create a peaceful haven by training honeysuckle up a simple arbor and placing a wooden seat underneath.*

● *Outdoor entertaining is made easier if you can gather your guests into a defined space. Create an eating area by paving a small space and erecting an awning or by making a change of level at one end of your garden.*

## STRUNG OUT

*No-one can deny that a modest amount of effort reaps its rewards in the garden, but in the heat of the day these tree-hung hammocks (above) invite the gardener to enjoy a well-earned rest.*

## A PLACE TO REST

*The painted table and chair and wrought iron bench (right) are attractive yet functional.*

# COUNTRY CROPS

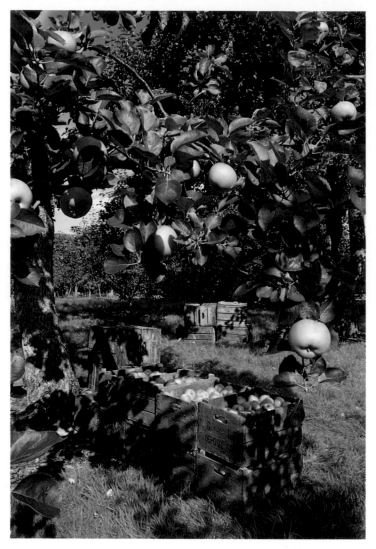

Supermarkets bring food fresh from the field, but by the time it has been transported, washed, graded and packaged, it tastes bland compared to food picked or plucked from the garden and carried direct to the kitchen table. Although our cottage predecessors found much of the necessary work of tilling, sowing, seeding and harvesting the land a time-consuming business, the quality of garden-fresh food was taken for granted by them.

Today those pleasures have been rediscovered and the kitchen garden has once again become a familiar feature. Divided into the traditional four plots by turf, brick or stone paths, crops are rotated around the plots to give their best

yield and protect against the build up of disease. In the past the harvest was limited; leeks, cabbage and kale in winter and beans, peas, onion and garlic augmented by the leaves of watercress, dandelion and lamb's lettuce in summer.

Nowadays a succession of brassicas, from cauliflowers to calabrese, follow legumes such as runner beans and peas which, in turn, follow the heavy-feeding potatoes, root crops and onions. Threads of marigolds and parsley, grown between crops of carrots help keep away unwelcome insects and brighten the beds, while cloches and cold frames extend the growing season. Salad crops of tomatoes and lettuce, grown amongst the ornamental borders, ensure an extended harvest of fresh food throughout the summer.

In old cottage gardens the herb bed grew alongside such useful flowers as the Apothecary's Rose (Rosa Gallica), which retained its scent when used as a pot-pourri, and peonies and clove-scented pinks, crushed into scented waters for sprinkling over washed linen and clothing. An additional source of food came from a stand of hazel or cob nuts, a quiet corner devoted to wild berries and from trees such as fig, olive or elder.

Today's gardens can be equally productive and pictures-que. Garden centres offer a bewildering choice of varieties and the new gardener should be guided by the same principles which influenced the work on the cottage itself, conserving what grows in the old neighbourhood rather than buying in precious, highly-bred species.

There has been a sad decline in growing cottage varieties of fruit trees. In England where once there were over 6,000 different apples, nine basic varieties now dominate. Old varieties were the rootstock of today's high-yield commercial breeds and famous varieties like the Bramley apple were developed in the kitchen garden. The Bramley was first sown by Mary Brailsford in her North England garden and given the name of the new cottage tenant, a Mr Bramley, when the tree bore fruit. Where an old trees still survives in the cottage garden it should be identified, pruned and, if possible, propagated. It may lack in yield, and a modest yield is sufficient for most households, but it will not lack in taste.

Every cottage has its own micro-climate in which one variety of vegetable will thrive while another will take ill and decline; a little research at the local café or inn should provide some homely advice on favoured varieties and will often result in a useful exchange of neighbourhood-grown seed. It is worth experimenting to find which readily available plants will grow easily in your soil, especially the more luxurious vegetables such as asparagus or squash, expensive to buy but surprisingly simple to cultivate, as long as the soil conditions are suitable.

Maintaining a good soil means maintaining a good compost heap. Situated in a shady corner where nothing else will grow, fed with kitchen waste, enriched with manure and filled out with grass clippings and leafmould, the humus-rich compost heap will do for the soil what no amount of dubious chemicals and expensive artificial fertilizers will achieve in a year of application.

A century ago, the prevailing sentiment of a family sitting down to eat what they had grown and raised for themselves was one of relief. These days it is more one of satisfaction. Apart from enjoying food whose production involved no unnecessary chemical short-cuts (and every gardener should consider growing crops without the use of pesticides and insecticides), there is a righteous pleasure in eating what you have cultivated yourself.

The cottager was kind to his land because he could not afford to be otherwise. Anyone seeking to re-establish a vegetable plot after it has been swamped by *les mauvaises herbes*, as the French so endearingly call the weeds, should make a series of trial diggings until they retrace the old, rich soil. Well treated, it will perform again and again. The cottage grounds should be planned out with as much attention to detail as is put into the house itself. Areas need to be allocated to fruit and flowers, and stockproof fences and weatherproof sheds provided for any animals. Layout will be dictated by the lie of the land, but a common model is to place flowers and lawns in the foreground, vegetables, washing line and the all-essential compost heap in the middle ground and the orchards and animal quarters, separated by a

*There is no mystery to growing a good crop of fruit; a well-fed soil and a good dose of sunshine are all anyone needs (opposite).*

*The right time to lift vegetables and herbs depends upon the season. Here (above) garlic, onions and lavender dry naturally in the sun.*

resolute and impenetrable fence, at the back of the grounds.

Within this arrangement there is room for a hive of bees, situated so that the flight path does not normally cross the garden path. And where the henhouse is close to the cottage, avoid keeping a cockerel: his summer morning call will anticipate the family alarm clock by several hours.

# HARVESTING AND PRESERVING

The golden rule for harvesting herbs, flowers and produce is the same; pick only the best, while it is at its best. Herbs and flowers should be picked at their peak and dried. Herbs like mint and marjoram, thyme and tarragon can be hung in bunches in a dry, airy shed alongside flowers such as lunaria with their silvery seed pods, yarrow, Chinese-lantern lillies and statice, cut before the flowers fully open. Others, like delphiniums, which keep their colours, can be picked and pressed. Sun, smoke, salt and ice were the traditional means of keeping food fresh and every autumn the cottage kitchen was a hive of activity: beans packed into brine-filled earthenware jars; dried peas placed in mice-proof tins; wire baskets filled with surplus eggs and steeped in buckets of waterglass; root vegetables lifted and stored in earth cellars or straw clamps; onions and garlic dried in the sun and hung in strings; apples cored and dried beside bunches of mint, oregano and lavender. Pots and pans bubbled with jams and chutneys, muslin bags hung from the legs of an upturned stool and dripped pink fruit liquids into china bowls ready for jelly making at the end of the day.

Before the advent of the food freezer, the business of food preservation was a serious cottage craft. Like other country crafts it had almost slipped into oblivion before people realized that the old techniques still have a role to play today.

In the past when the housewife had filled her final earthenware storage jar and placed it with the others on the pantry shelf, she could breath a sigh of relief and begin preparations for that other ancient method of preserving the natural qualities of fruit, the making of wines and ciders for the following season.

The fermenting of alcohol by any other than commercial means is another neglected craft. At one time each country region made its own distinctive brews such as the *eau de vie* of France, Irish *potsheen*, American applejack and the country wines of England. Many traditional recipes were outlawed and lost, only to be replaced by synthetic, sweetened commercial substitutes: a sure measure of the loss is to spend some time with a neighbourly farmer who still keeps a few bottles by for guests.

Although a productive garden in a good year is like an unstoppable flood of food, people today have little time to wholeheartedly follow all the old methods of preserving. The solution is to pursue quality rather than quantity, to stock the freezer with a tray of French beans and peas and to line the pantry shelves with a modest selection of pickled beetroot, shallots, fruit chutneys and relishes. Onions, when sun-dried, can be stored in the legs of old tights, surplus fruit can be pulped and frozen and, mindful of waistlines, low-sugar jams can be made and refrigerated until needed.

## HARVESTING HERBS AND FLOWERS

*A native of southern Europe, lavender epitomizes perfect country garden produce, not least because it has been neglected over the years (right).*

*Pick flowers such as poppies (above) as soon as they begin to fade then hang them upside down in a warm place to dry.*

# INDEX

arbor 116, 120, 130
arch, garden 120

baskets 65, 80
bathroom
    beams 110
    condensation 110
    damp-proofing 110
    display 106
    floor 106
    history of 106
    planning 110–11
    storage 106, 111
    tiles 108
    walls 106, 108
beams
    bathroom 110
    chamfered 16
    dating a building from 16
    treatment of 68, 70
bedding 96–7
bedrooms 89–103
    beds 76, 94–7
    history of 89, 90
    layout 92–3
    quilts 98
    soft furnishings 100
    storage 102
beds
    American field 100
    American wooden 96
    box/cupboard 94
    cot, North European 96
    half-headed/stump 94
    mattresses 94
    metal bedstead 94, 96
    press bedstead 94
    rope bunk 94
    settle 94, 96
    tester (four-poster) 100,
        102
    truckle 94
beehive 135
brick
    cottage 35
    handmade 16
    infill 35

Roman 16
    wall 70

charnel 90
clapboard buildings 21, 27, 35
clootie 84
cob (earth) cottage 22
colour treatment 70–3
    see also paint; painted exteriors
commemorative inscriptions
    17
compost heap 135
conservatory 123, 124
    eating area as 124
    frost-sensitive plants for 123
    garden extension as 124
    living space as 124
cooking utensils 45, 49, 50
cooling house 17
corn dollies 84
cottage setting 20, 24–5
crafts & textiles 84–7
croft, Hebridean 15
croglofft, Welsh 90
crop rotation 134
Cumbrian cot 12
curtains 28
    bathroom 108
    bedroom 100
    café 82
    door 82
    living room 84

damp-proofing 22
    bathroom 110
    floors 40
    see also waterproofing
datestones 17
Devon cottage 34, 49
dining room see eating areas
display
    bathroom 106
    kitchen 50
    living room 86
door handles & knockers 32
doorhood 35
doors

cart 17
Celtic customs 33
Greek 38
heck (stable) 32
history of 32
ledge & brace 22, 32
low 38
repair of 32
Scandinavian 38
studded oak 22
vertically divided 32, 37
doorways 16, 32–3

eating areas
    dining room 56
    kitchen 52–3
    outside 56, 57, 127, 130
estate journals 17
extension 19, 35
exteriors
    building materials 7, 8, 10, 11,
        14–15, 16
    painted 26–7, 104–5
    restoring 20–1

firebacks, decoration of 74
firebox & grate 74
fireplaces
    fire-resistant elm, use of 74
    hearth, position of 15, 74
    lintel (bressumer) 74
    mantelpiece 74
    material of 45, 74
    restoration of 68
    see also stoves
flint cottage 25, 35
floor
    bathroom 106
    boards 40
    damp-proofing 40
    earth 40
    flattening dance 40
    stone flags 40
    terracotta tiles 40
floor coverings 40, 84
flowers, drying of 138
fresco 105

fruit trees, cottage 134
fuel stoves 25
furniture, traditional country
    court cupboard 76
    dresser 49, 50, 54, 76, 86
    history of 76
    'seize' 76
    settle bed 76
    see also painted furniture

garden, cottage 113–30
    dividers 25, 116, 120, 130
    history of 114
    layout 116
    planting 24, 118
garden furniture
    chairs 126, 130
    hammocks 130
    table 130
    weatherproof 130
garden path 20, 22, 116, 134
gutters 21, 22

half-timbering 11, 25, 35
hall furniture 38
hall house 16
hallways
    floor 36, 37
    history of 35
    lighting 36
    orientation 36
    walls 36, 37
harvesting 138
herbs 136–7
    culinary 136
    harvesting of 136
    medicinal 114, 136
    planting of 136
    shade-loving 136
history, cottage 16, 17, 104
hopkiln 17, 28
horse-brasses 84

ingle-nook 44, 74, 86
inn 16

kitchen
  display 50
  eating areas 52
  furniture 44, 46, 52, 54
  history of 49
  layout 46
  storage 49
kitchen garden 20, 34–5

laundry 62
limestone houses 8, 10, 26
livestock
  dairy produce 140
  dovecot/*pigeonnier* 140
  living quarters 66, 140
  pigsty 140
  poultry 140
living room
  beams 66
  display 86
  history of 66
  partition walls 66
  soft furnishings 80
local landscapes 114
local materials 14–15
log cabin 8, 10, 22, 27
loggia 56–7
longhouse 34, 35, 66

maps, early 17
mats 84
microclimate 135

nut trees 134

outdoor rooms
  aspect, southerly 126
  eating in 127
  floors 127
  furniture 57, 126
  porch 127
  terrace 126
  trellis 126
  veranda 127
  wall vents 127
outhouses 17, 24, 62

paint
  colour 70–3, 104–5
  design 105
  distemper 104–5
  lead 26
  permeable
painted exteriors 19, 26–7,
  104–5
  *see also* whitewash
painted furniture 43, 78–9,
  103
parish records 17
partition wall, removal of 45,
  52, 66
pergola 120
pests 134
pipes, external 24
pitching eyes 28
plant containers 24, 122, 123
plants
  climbers 24, 25, 120
  frost-sensitive 123
  history of 120
  rotation of 117
  thinning out 118
  wild 117
plasterboarding 68
porch 24, 34–5
  hood 35
preserving
  alcohol, fermenting of 138
  jams 138
  pickles 138
  sun-dried onions 138

quilts
  bridal 98, 99
  clothing 98, 99
  design 99
  embroidery 99
  laying out of the dead 98

restoration
  exterior 20–1
  original features 17, 68, 105
roof tiles
  clay 17

  dark slate 16
  green slate 12
  Roman 12
  slurried slate 7
  stone slate 17
  *tuile à canal* 12
roofs
  beehive 15
  cat slide 62
  construction 16, 66, 90
  half-hipped 11
  shingle 21, 28, 34
  thatch 8, 15, 17, 19, 21, 27
  *see also* roof tiles
rugs 84

sgraffito 27
Shaker 8, 49, 56, 80, 84
shutters
  decorated 30
  hanging of 30
  history of 28
  louvred 30
  painted 25, 27, 30
sink, kitchen 46
soft furnishings
  bedroom 100
  living room 80–5
  textiles 84
stencilling
  floors 40
  furniture 44, 78
storey 16, 34
stoves
  'American' 74
  Scandinavian 74
  tiled 78
  wood-burning 46, 68, 74

television aerials 25
tiles
  bathroom 108
  dining area 56
  kitchen 45
  *see also* roof tiles
timber-frame buildings 8, 11, 12,
  14, 25, 35

tongue-and-groove panelling,
  106, 108
trellis 24, 25, 35, 120, 126
*trompe-l'oeil* 70, 89

utility room 45, 62

vegetables 134–5
veranda *see* porch
vernacular
  buildings 12, 14, 15
  design 76
  features 11, 28
  furnishings 14, 65

wall
  bathroom 106, 108
  cupboard 49
  internal 68
  knocking through 45, 52, 66
  tongue-and-groove panelling
  106, 108
wall clock 30
wall surfaces
  painting 70–3
  plaster 70
  preparation of 70
  rubble 73
  timber 70
waterproofing 21
  *see also* damp-proofing
wattle & daub 26, 68
weaving gallery 16
whipple house 21
whitewash 7, 10, 12, 19, 21, 28,
  37, 56, 104
window
  dormer 8, 11, 90
  frame 26, 28
  glazed 28
  history of 28
  lead-painted 26
  Mediterranean 27
  repair of 28
  sash 28
  size of 16, 27, 28
  *see also* shutters

# ACKNOWLEDGMENTS

## AUTHOR'S ACKNOWLEDGMENTS

The author is indebted to Joanna Bradshaw, David Laws, Mandy Little, Annik Marsollier, Simon Mole, Jean Perry, Catherine and David Petts, Michelle Seddon-Harvey and Vivienne Southorn.

The publisher thanks the following photographers and organizations for their kind permission to reproduce the photographs in this book:

*1* S & O Mathews; *2* Stylograph/Yves Duronsoy/Helene Laforgue; *3* S & O Mathews; *4* Andrew Lawson; *5* Stylograph/ Jacques Dirand; *6–7* Reflections Photo Library/Jennie Woodcock; *7* John Heseltine; *8 left* Serge Chirol; *8–9* Jessie Walker; *10* Christian Sarramon; *11* Explorer/M. Smith; *12 above* Explorer/A. Philippon; *12 centre* Paul Ryan/International Interiors; *12 below* Explorer/S. Grandadam; *13* Michael Busselle; *14 above* Ffotograff/ Patricia Aithie; *14 below* Explorer/N. Thibaut; *15 above* Serge Chirol; *15 below* Edifice/Hart Davies; *16 above* John Miller; *16 below* S & O Mathews; *17* Michael Busselle; *18–19* Clay Perry; *19* Hamish Parks; *20* Ianthe Ruthven; *21* Edifice/Gillian Darley; *22 left* Michael Busselle; *22 right* Andrew Lawson; *23* Jessie Walker; *24 above* Christian Sarramon; *24 below* Jerry Harpur (Chiffchaffs, Dorset); *25* S & O Mathews; *26 above* Explorer/P. Roy; *26 below* Explorer/F. Jalain; *27 above left* Explorer/S. Cordier; *27 below left* John Miller; *29* Ingalill Snitt; *30 above* John Miller; *30 below left* Explorer/B. Maltaverne; *30 below right* Explorer/P. Roy; *31* Elizabeth Whiting & Associates/David George/Cassell; *32 left* Guy Bouchet; *32 right* Ffotograff/Patricia Aithie; *33* Christian Sarramon; *34* © Image/Dennis Krukowski, 'The Farmhouse', Bantam Books, USA; *35 above left* Elizabeth Whiting & Associates/ Jerry Harpur; *35 below left* Jan Baldwin; *35 right* Jessie Walker; *36* Simon McBride; *37 left* Simon McBride; *37 right* Ianthe Ruthven; *38 above left* Agence Top/Pascal Chevallier; *38 above right* Marie Claire Maison/Limbour/Billaud; *38 below left* Pia Tryde; *38 below right* Guy Bouchet; *38–9* © Image/Dennis Krukowski, 'The Farmhouse', Bantam Books, USA; *40* Ianthe Ruthven; *40 below* Amparo Garrido; *41* Paul Ryan/JB Visual Press; *42–3* Peter Woloszynski; *43* Gary Rogers; *44* Daniel & Emmanuelle Minassian; *45* Elle Decoration/Simon Wheeler; *46 above* Tim Beddow; *46 below left* Christine Ternynck; *46 below right* Christian Sarramon; *47* Jeff McNamara; *48 above* Marie Claire Maison/ Bailhache/Comte; *48 below left* Antoine Rozes; *48 below centre* Fritz von der Schulenburg (Villa Vicosa); *48 below right* Simon McBride; *49* Kari Haavisto; *50* Elizabeth Whiting & Associates/Tim Street-Porter; *51 above* Elizabeth Whiting & Associates/Spike Powell; *51 below left* Marie Claire Idées/Chabaneix/Chabaneix/ Bastit; *51 below centre* Christian Sarramon; *51 below right* Agence Top/Pascal Chevallier (courtesy of Michel Sauboua, Director Epsilen Gallery, Lyon, France); *52* Simon McBride; *53* Explorer/ L. Girard; *54–55* Bent Rej; *56* Marie Claire Maison/Bailhache/ Comte; *56 below* Gary Rogers; *57* Ianthe Ruthven; *58 left* Karen Bussolini; *58 right* Amparo Garrido; *59* Derry Moore; *60–61* Marie Claire Maison/Chabaneix/Ardouin; *62 left* Ianthe Ruthven; *62 right* Walter Smalling Jnr; *63* Jean-Pierre Godeau; *64–5* Tim Beddow; *65* Jean-Pierre Godeaut; *67* Simon McBride; *68* Christian Sarramon; *69* Guy Bouchet; *70* Jean-Pierre Godeaut; *71* Tim Beddow; *72* Amparo Garrido; *73 above* Ianthe Ruthven; *73 below left* Marie Claire Maison/Snitt/Rozensztroch; *73 below right* Deidi von Schaewen; *75 above* Simon McBride; *75 below left* Elizabeth Whiting & Associates/Spike Powell; *76 left* Ingalill Snitt; *76 right* Derry Moore; *77* Derry Moore; *78* Stylograph/ Jacques Dirand; *79* Elizabeth Whiting & Associates/David George/Cassell; *80–1* World of Interiors/Tim Beddow; *82* Hannu Mannynoksa/JB Visual Press; *83* Boys Syndication/ Michael Boys; *85* Elizabeth Whiting & Associates/Anaya; *86* Simon McBride; *87* Walter Smalling Jnr; *88–89* Marie Claire Maison/Snitt/Puech/Rozensztroch; *89* David Phelps; *91* Amparo Garrido; *92 above* Paul Ryan/JB Visual Press; *92 below* Christian Sarramon; *93 above* Antoine Rozes; *93 below* Jean-Pierre Godeaut; *96* Jessie Walker; *96 below left* Lars Hallen/Design Press; *96 below right* Paul Ryan/International Interiors; *97 above* Deidi von Schaewen; *97 below left* Ianthe Ruthven; *97 below right* Stylograph/ Jacques Dirand; *98 above* Ianthe Ruthven; *98 below* Arcaid/Richard Bryant; *99* Walter Smalling Jnr; *100 above* Boys Syndication/ Michael Boys; *100 below left* John Miller; *100 below right* Houses & Interiors/Simon Butcher; *101* Paul Ryan/JB Visual Press; *102* Jerome Darblay; *103* Paul Ryan/JB Visual Press; *104–105* Simon McBride; *106* Marie Claire Maison/Chabaneix/Chabaneix/Bastit; *107* Deidi von Schaewen; *108–109* House & Interiors/Simon Butcher; *110 left* Simon McBride; *110 right* Houses & Interiors/Ed Buziak; *111 left* Christian Sarramon; *111 right* Houses & Interiors/ Simon Butcher; *112–113* Marianne Majerus; *113* Elizabeth Whiting & Associates/Marie O'Hara; *115* Arcaid/Richard Bryant (Mr Baker's garden); *116 above* S & O Mathews; *116 below* Jerry Harpur (Dolwen, Llanrhaedr-ym-Mochnant, Powys); *117 above* Andrew Lawson; *117 below* Gary Rogers; *118–9* S & O Mathews; *121* Jerry Harpur (Designer: Bruce Kelly, New York); *122 left* Amparo Garrido; *122 right* Deidi von Schaewen; *123 left* Marijke Heuff (Mr & Mrs Heymans Christiaans); *123 right* Gary Rogers; *124 above* Amparo Garrido; *124 below* Ingalill Snitt; *125 above* Dia Press; *125 below* Agence Top/Pascal Chevallier; *127* Fritz von der Schulenburg (Robert Kime); *128–129* Agence Top/Pierre Hussenot; *130* Yves Duronsoy; *131* Brigitte Thomas; *132–133* John Miller; *133* Elizabeth Whiting & Associates/Di Lewis; *134* S & O Mathews; *135* Gary Rogers; *136* IMP/Marie-Louise Avery; *137* Andrew Lawson; *138* S & O Mathews; *139* Brigitte Thomas; *140 above* Serge Chirol; *140 centre* Simon McBride; *140 below* S & O Mathews; *141* Christian Sarramon; *142–3* Design Press/Lars Hallen; *144* Agence Top/Pascal Chevallier.